I Know This Looks Bad

I Know This Looks Bad

Errors and Graces in a Louche Life

BY

JPV OLIVER, GENT

Epigraph Books
Rhinebeck, New York

Hardcover ISBN: 978-1-954744-27-1
eBook ISBN: 978-1-954744-28-8

Library of Congress Control Number: 2021911767

Book design by Colin Rolfe

Author photo by Vincent Giordano

Photographs are the property of the author, are in the public
domain or are used by permission.

Epigraph Books
epigraphps.com

This book is dedicated to my three adult children,
John Joseph, Emily MacGowan and Mary Elgin,
people of real accomplishment and unbounded kindness

and to

Leesa Perazzo whom I love foreverly.

"In that book, which is my memory,
On the first page of the chapter that is the day when I
    first met you,
Appear the words,
'Here begins a new life'."
                                        — Dante Alighieri, *Vita Nuova*, 1295

ACKNOWLEDGMENTS

Marcy Brucellaria, a friend from GE Capital days, edited my deathless prose. She was eagle-eyed, tireless and biblically patient. *Lapsus calami* are of course mine alone.

The following individuals gave freely of their time and intellects and, though I am deeply grateful for their help, they bear no responsibility for what follows.

They are Ron Atkinson, Dr Albena Azmanova, John Barry, Peter Barry, Esq, Bette Bono, Esq, Tom Carson, Dr Roselle Chartock, Chiwan Choi, Maureen Cleary, Dr Cathy Colt, Labkhand Dadyar, Pete Duval, Michael Eck, John Glatt, Nancy Hass, Tarquin Henderson, Ken Jacobs, Amen Kahwajy, Susan Kipp, Mahabanoo Mody-Kotwal, Marissa Lambrinos, Janice Landrum, Will Levith, Barbara Lippert, Richard Lovrich, Ruth Marshall, Lia Matera, Lorna Mellon, Susan Mihalic, Hamish Montgomery, Tony Paredes, Deirdre Peterson, Dr Roger Pomerantz, Pip Pullen, Virginia Randall, Tamara Rosenberg, Poupak Sepehri, Dr Lee Shapiro, Gary Sheffer, Hedwig Stallings, Lucian K Truscott IV, Bernard Klein Wassink, Juliana Ratner Wheeler and Daniel Whitney.

"Times are bad. Children no longer obey their parents and everyone is writing a book."

— Cicero, 43 BCE

Praeludium

My life isn't unique, but in some ways it has been singular – like yours, I reckon.

My parents, John Oliver, a beer distributor, and Winifred Smith, an impoverished war widow, met at a 1953 bowling banquet in the textile mill town of Amsterdam, New York, the tatty burg where I was likely conceived. They married in March of that year and I arrived in September in the usual manner.

Students of nuptial norms and human gestation will note a squiggle in the timeline. I was the giddy-up around their wedding and, whilst one might prefer a more posh origin story, this is where we find ourselves.

The Oliver ancestral manse at 82 Osborne Road, West Albany, where we lived, featured an above-ground pool, an ice-skating rink, an upright player piano, a regular piano, a drum kit, a classic Lionel train set, an ancient leather-pocket slate pool table, a fully-stocked bar in the cellar (*The Oliver's* boasted the neon sign because grammarians were in short supply) and a vast collection of kitsch. The house itself was encased in pink aluminum siding my father bought with 300 cases of beer from his distributorship.

The place was of course dubbed The Pink Palace. Tours available seven days a week.

After a secondary education *à l'Ecole Militaire*, I drove one of my father's two beer trucks. Viewing my work as a beer man, he urged college, which I attended in Indiana and then graduate school at the University of Kent at Canterbury, England.

Viewing my work as a scholar, my graduate advisor

urged anything other than academia. I did what I could and it wasn't really anybody's fault.

At 26, I returned to America to become public relations director for The New York State Nurses Association, a labor union and professional organization of 37,000 RNs.

Soon after I signed on, 5,500 NYSNA union members walked out of New York City hospitals in a wildly illegal job action and I was dispatched to Manhattan to organize a huge press conference in one of the world's most fractious media markets. A baptism of fire really.

Getting off the train from Albany, I strode down the gangway in the fetid heat of Grand Central. At the end, a woman held a microphone and a sign with my name on it and, next to her, a guy balanced a huge contraption on his shoulder. Emblazoned with WNBC NEW YORK in big blue letters, it was one of TV's first live mini-cams in America.

Microphone Lady fired tough questions at me about heartless, money-grubbing nurses abandoning desperately sick babies and the elderly.

Through sheer luck, I acknowledged her questions and explained why the RNs took such a drastic step. That, as it happens, is *precisely* how you take control of a hostile interview. The whole thing went out instantly to tens of thousands of viewers, a good opening for a budding propagandist.

Most of my work-life was spent as a speechwriter, media relations operative and dogsbody at a disease foundation, a big PR consultancy, then Seagram and GE Capital.

Confronted with a potential layoff in 1993, I donned Elizabethan raiment and went to my son's second grade class to talk about Shakespeare. I then wrote a funny piece about the experience for **Newsweek** in the desperate hope a national audience might result in remunerative and secure employ.

That Hail Mary pass worked and, as a result, I spent nearly 20 years at GE. But hoo boy, that was close.

What follows are commentaries I've penned on social media over the last 10 years – 365 of them in fact. That seems like an awful lot, but my wife, Leesa, had a really good reason for including them which I can't remember right now.

In the book-writing dodge, what you're reading is called a modular memoir, a set of individual entries meant to create a cohesive mosaic. You get to decide if I succeeded.

Most are epigrams. Short and sweet, epigrams work because readers have better things to do, but subject-wise, mine are all over the place. Those seeking organic unity, piety, patience, organization and trenchant insights are encouraged to seek elsewhere.

With a few exceptions, I avoid politics. Encounters with celebrities are included because meeting them was memorable – certainly more for me than them. I have my metaphorical way with these people, but I don't exaggerate or malign unnecessarily. Honestly, most were swell and anyway they can't sue because they're dead or close to it.

Some entries are about long-ago family members, including my beloved father. These people were so exceptionally kind to me when I was small, I felt I owed them something. There is, however, little mention of my mother, a troubled woman on whom I choose not to dwell.

Over the last 10 years, readers have been encouraging, enthusiastic even, about some of my work, but really what do they know? They have however been gracious, witty and creative friends and I'm lucky to have them.

In the text, sometimes spelling, punctuation and word-choices are in American English and sometimes British English. I wrote in both for university and for work and I still do.

A decade ago, I created a character called JPV Oliver, Gent, an overweening snob who's posh, eccentric, deeply ridiculous and who drinks too much. He bears no resemblance to me, apart from his breathtaking affectations, Victorian vocabulary, flatulence, pretentiousness, mild obesity, poor eyesight, overweening snobbery and excessive consumption of Laphroaig.

JPV Oliver, Gent, is aided and abetted by his devoted longtime valet, Finial Horan, who also serves as butler and chauffer. Other members of the inner circle appear anon.

My real name is John Oliver and I spend hours explaining I'm not the HBO guy and I'm not English (affectations notwithstanding). I also use JPV Oliver, Gent, here to make clear this book has nothing to do with the hugely talented comedian with whom I share a name. I had the moniker first, but HBO's probably got snippy lawyers whom I don't wish to meet.

The late American TV newsman Harry Reasoner wrote a memoir called **Before the Colors Fade**. This was ironic for somebody who spent most of his life in black and white, but it's a lovely idea when you've got more yesterdays than tomorrows.

Shakespeare of course talks about the seven ages of man and, so far, I've done five of them. I'm currently full of wise saws and modern instances – and, if encouraged, a sigh like a furnace can still be summoned. My age at this writing, 67, certainly isn't the end of what Will called a man's "strange eventful history", but you can see it from where I sit.

Happily, the colours are still vivid.

I'm delighted you're here and I ask you charge your glasses. If you don't like the page you're on, try another one. I mean, some of this stuff is good.

JPV Oliver, Gent
Saratoga Springs, New York
New Year's Day 2021

January 1 **Bathroom Humor**

Last summer, I locked myself in a men's room stall at The Saratoga Casino Hotel. The stall door was stuck; normal egress was not happening. An attempted low-crawl beneath the divider was unsavory and unsuccessful.

Plangent cell phone calls followed unanswered shouts. An executive at said business was dispatched to rescue me. Let's call him Carl because that's his name. If you rang Central Casting and asked for Clark Kent, you'd get Carl. Tall, strong, chiseled jaw, Hollywood handsome, you could park a Buick on his chin. He had golf-hardened arms. He was laconic. If he sported a cape, you'd go, Yeah, OK.

"John, you in there?" Carl asked.

"Why yes, as it happens, I am, Carl," I replied snottily.

"You OK?"

"No," I whined. "I've been locked for an hour in a fetid fucking stall in an un-air conditioned 60-year-old men's room on the hottest day of the year."

"Stop whining. Step away from the door."

As I did this, Carl kicked the door in with a blast from his mighty leg causing the metal lock to fly like a Hellfire missile inches from my head. Still, freedom was at hand. When I said that, having saved my life, in some cultures he'd now own me, Carl's manly expression changed not at all.

January 2   Relief from Above

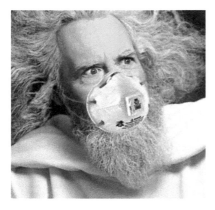

During the height of The Plague, the Pope asked God to stop the murderous Plague that killed 2.5 million people around the world, so that was a big help.

Fact: God started the pandemic on New Year's Day, 2020, because He was desperately hung-over and in a shitty mood. He was angry because The Virgin Mary wasn't talking to Him.

The night before, making dinner, She got into the cooking sherry and actually screamed, "Who died and left you God?" Since then, She's been staying at her mom's. Jesus is no help, what with His video games, fat blunts and Busch Light all day and night. A celestial shit show, I tell you.

January 3   An Innocent Abroad

My ex has wealthy relatives who live in Bilbao, Spain. We once gathered our young children and hurtled eastward across the Atlantic, Iberia Airlines business class, to visit. I learned five things on that junket.

First, three maids – two for the day and one in the evening – wash, iron and fold your dress shirts so flawlessly, you don't want them touched ever again. Second, there's a giant topiary outside the Guggenheim Museum in the shape of a puppy. The locals call it *Poopie* and don't find this the least bit funny. Third, on a crowded, chaotic domestic coach flight in Spain, your children are annoyed. "What's wrong with this plane?" they demand. Fourth, if you say "the Basque Region" and not "the Basque Country", the Basque get cranky.

And lastly, Bilbao's proper name – and this is true – is William J Bao IV.

January 4 ## Don't Break Your Meat

New scholarly research out of Europe suggests William Shakespeare may have smoked pot. That would explain the Earl of Kent's remarks in **King Lear**, Act 2, Scene 2: "A knave, a rascal, an eater of broken meats*. A man who liketh the weed o' the striped rodent... Thou bongth?"

* In Elizabethan English, "meats" referred exclusively to pepperoni pizza. "Broken" means leftover or cold the morning after. Shakespeare scholarship is one of my core competencies.

January 5 ## A Lost Boy

The thing I remember about 1995 Romania is the ancient gnarled forest just beyond the ring road of Bucuresti Airport. Gnarled as a dark fairytale, a place for ugly crimes, that forest was a place of haunting secrets. The trees were medieval grey, not a proper colour for trees.

The entire Serbian airline, all five brand-new Boeing 767s, was parked in a clearing behind concertina wire – the Americans couldn't bomb them in Romania. The greetings and the smiles were warm in Bucharest, but things were not OK.

January 6   **Seatmate**

Billie Jean King is one of the greatest players in the history of tennis. She's also a devoted gay woman who's done much for the LGBTQ+ cause. She and I slept together. Explanation follows.

We were seated next to one another on a commercial flight to Europe on a long ago January night. Knowing nothing of sports, let alone women's tennis, I kept to myself as we hurtled westward. She fell asleep and her head lolled on my shoulder. Soon I slept too. Years later, I bumped into Ms King in a Manhattan TV studio. We were introduced and shook hands, whereupon I brightly noted our history. "I'm really sure we haven't slept together," she said laughing. "Oh yes we have," I retorted. The room went deathly quiet. When I revealed she'd drooled on my shirt, hilarity ensued.

January 7   **Spit Take**

I toiled in the wine trade for a decade. In the wine cellar – on the 7th floor of the Seagram building high above Park Avenue – one would gently decant, say, a '64 *Margaux*, nose it, sip, taste, then spit into a specially designed receptacle. You were meant to discern all that was going on in that glass and describe it with precision.

But how artfully one spat, how contained, how fast and accurate, how strong, how narrow the stream, mattered too. Cool spitters were admired and I dubbed one fellow, famous for his technique, Great Expectorations.

January 8

Grasp Exceeded

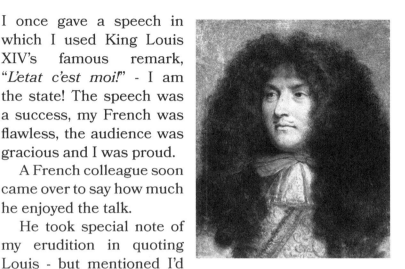

I once gave a speech in which I used King Louis XIV's famous remark, *"L'etat c'est moi!"* - I am the state! The speech was a success, my French was flawless, the audience was gracious and I was proud.

A French colleague soon came over to say how much he enjoyed the talk.

He took special note of my erudition in quoting Louis - but mentioned I'd actually said, "I am the tea!"

Yet another triumph on the international stage.

January 9

Soubriquet de Jour

I'm not the sort of person who gets nicknames, still I have a few. My mother named me The Prince. We didn't get on and it was not a term of affection. Jock, a typical Scottish given name, was applied to me because I'm the antithesis of an athlete. Since I'm occasionally debauched, Champagne Johnny was in vogue for a time. Johnny Ollie is a recent one, as is my favorite, J Bubbs, echoic of bubbles in the champers. After my second COVID vaccine shot, I became Johnny Two Jabs.

January 10   **You Can Quote Me**

In *l'Ecole Militaire*, the yearbook editors chose a quote to describe each graduating cadet. For me, they used a line from Hamlet, "A politician, one who might circumvent

God". I thought this apt.

Avoiding God's no problem since He does not exist. The IRS and HM's Revenue and Customs, by contrast, are stickier wickets. In the photo, I'm third from the right.

January 11   **TGIF**

As I dressed today, *après ma douche*, I had occasion to sit firmly on the substantial brass buckle of my belt. I promise this is not as erotically rewarding as it may seem. It was then necessary to upbraid my valet, Finial, for his carelessness. I didn't cane the poor bugger because such is frowned upon in our soulless epoch, but I thought about it. Finial is pictured trying manfully to operate the blower in the upstairs corridor. His buttling is uneven at best.

January 12   **Land of Steady Habits**

Connecticut, where I lived for 20 years, is mainly a place where rich people play golf. The more *outré* play tennis, but those people went to state schools and are therapists who spend their lives treating "The Well and Wealthy".

Many Nutmeggers, which is what you call the people who live there, have pools attended by well-muscled pool boys named Raoul. Raouls are very popular in Connecticut. The purpose of the pool is for you to float in while you sip a gin and tonic and look at your huge boat parked in the driveway. A lot of bored housewives prefer to look at Raoul.

January 13   **Antimacassar is the Word**

The word *flâneur* is resurgent. My first such saunter was as a lad of 15 in Paris. I wore an ascot for the occasion which my new friend, Yvette, fancied.

The scales fell from my Upstate New York eyes in a Parisian minute. Over the years, other cities hove into view, but their *arrondissements* were quotidian by contrast. Other women showed up too, but Yvette was not a *jeune femme* so easily forgotten. Today, I'm rocking an ascot (Br Eng: cravat) in her honour. We *flâneures* have our rituals.

January 14 # For the Way We Were

A typical Facebook affinity group is "[Your City or Town Name Here]: The Way We Were". Such groups have common tropes.

- "Who remembers twirling on the lunch counter seats at Fishbein's Drug Store till you puked?"
- "Here's a 1962 photo of Sister Euthanasia's 1st grade class at Holy Woodchipper Catholic School. Can you find me?"; and,
- "Friday nites at Ted's Fish Fry on Central Ave was heaven."

Depart from the turgid formula and admins and readers rain imprecations various down on you. For example, I just got my peepee whacked by "Saratoga: Then and Now" because I said residents of a low-income public housing facility are "bootless and unhorsed". I was dubbed arrogant, rude, pompous, cruel, etc, so they must have talked to my ex-wife. Can you find me in the picture below?

January 15   Hero?

My New Year's resolution – to not eat ice cream out of the carton with a shoehorn whilst sporting tatty, greying underpants and standing, shivering, in my darkened kitchen at three am, listening to **Long Cool Woman in a Black Dress** by The Hollies – held firm for 14 triumphant, glory-soaked days. We're now at *status quo ante*, but what a madcap, hell's-a-poppin' thrill ride it was.

January 16   Bay Doors Open, Lieutenant

After World War II, the US and UK conducted The Allied Bombing Survey to understand the results of the air war against Germany. It was led by John Kenneth Galbraith, one of the great minds of the 20th Century. At one point, they interviewed an old woman outside Frankfurt. "You blew up my house, leveled my town, nearly killed my brother, terrified us for months and now you want to know how I liked it?"

The survey showed that American and British bombs actually increased German weapons production. The attacks focused on city centres freeing up workers to go to the suburban factories, which were then able to operate 24 hours a day. The US Army Air Corps and RAF were none too pleased at the findings.

January 17

Bring Your $s to Saratoga Springs

Try Glassblowing.
July 4th – Labor Day
at The Gideon Putnam Hotel

An early settler called Gideon Putnam is the reason this once little village in the middle of nowhere has a huge main street with big wide sidewalks. He founded the place and saw its future as a tourist town. He believed we'd need to have room to turn all the carriages around, an eventuality he foresaw in 1810.

January 18

Doing Good

I volunteered at a nonprofit event in Saratoga today. One of the volunteers, an Englishwoman, came out of the restroom and announced,

"We need loo rolls," British English for toilet paper. But I thought she said "Lou Rawls" and I said, "What the hell do you need a R&B singer in the bathroom for? Besides, he's dead".

She responded with, "Loo rolls can't die".

"Oh, yes he can – 2006 I think. You'll Never Find Another Love Like Mine."

"I don't need a love like yours, you wanker. I just need loo rolls," her patience fraying. "You know, bumf. You do speak English, right?"

"Fine," I said. "We'll just have to get some imitator or something."

"What's imitation toilet paper, for god sakes?" she snarled marching away.

Foreigners am I right?

January 19   # Boaty McBoatface

In 1996, I was the protocol officer for the very American CEO of GE Capital's grand reception aboard HMY Britannia, on the docks at Palm Beach Harbor.

My efforts as a protocol officer set the practice of diplomacy back 150 years.

HRH Prince Philip was of course as effortlessly charming as you'd expect. He gave us a tour of the yacht's private quarters and his stateroom, which he largely designed. That evening, a gala black tie dinner was laid on at The Breakers.

Three hundred Palm Beach Socialites attended the glittering affair which was the hottest ticket that season. The CEO sat to HRH's right. I sat next to my boss in case translation was required.

> CEO [Trying to chat up HRH]: "GE Capital has a huge presence in Britain."
> HRH [Gazing at his consommé]: "Quite."
> CEO [Still trying]: "Maybe we could connect with some government economic ministers."
> HRH [Not looking up from his consommé]: "I never think about business."
> Drunk Congressman's Wife Across The Table: "I think it's so awful waz happen to yer kids [Charles and Diana's divorce], cause the same thing's happenin' to our kids too...".

It was a long dinner during which one heard only slurps.

January 20   # NASA Says

The New York Post reports NASA will remove names of some celestial bodies because they may be offensive. The Eskimo nebula and the Siamese Twins Galaxy are going, as is The Trump University Black Hole. The Milky Way is now the Organic Skim Lactose-Free 2% Milky Way. Uranus remains untouched.

January 21   # Adventures in Publicity

My PR efforts at Seagram were high-minded, artful and cerebral. One idea I had was a giant greeting card that you walked into to sign, another was a giant bowling ball and bowling pins. The latter nearly took out the showroom of a Chicago Cadillac dealership. My psychiatrist felt the symbolism of these stunts related directly to my quote unquote issues.

January 22   NiceNet

The founder of the Boy Scouts, Lord Robert Baden-Powell (1857 - 1941), is legendary for his work as a spy for His Majesty. He toiled in what would become MI-6, the British intelligence service, often traveling disguised as a butterfly collector. Nothing odd there. CIA used to send congratulatory postcards to newly-minted Eagle Scouts. Baden-Powell would have loved that.

Clockwise from top right: Berlin Wall, Memorial Wall, Statue of General William Donovan, Aerial View of CIA Compound, and Entrance to the Original Headquarters Building.

We regret we will no longer provide certificates of congratulations to new Eagle Scouts. Due to the demands of recent events, we have curtailed some activities in order for us to concentrate on the War on Terrorism.

Sincerely,

Molly Hale

Molly Hale
Central Intelligence Agency Public Communications
Washington, DC 20505
www.cia.gov

January 23   Where's the Men's Room

I devoted much of my work life to two corporations, Seagram and GE Capital. Human beauty, geniality, genius, venality, lust, kindness and stupidity in these enterprises were not in greater supply than in the population at large, despite the excessive incidence of Ivy League, INSEAD and Oxbridge MBAs. Highly educated men and women used words like Throughput, *Tranche*, Supply Chain, Matrices, Win-Win, *Di Minimis* and Action Plan. My boss even said Stochastic once, but, in fairness, he'd had a glass of Malbec which provokes gibberish. You and your 401k may be similarly situated. If you're unhappy in your corporate job, just dial nine to get out.

January 24 **Lead, Follow Or**

 I was a little boy in the run-up to the 1962 Cuban missile crisis and I remember asking my father why we weren't getting a bomb shelter in our yard like my friend's family. "You've got to have faith," he said quietly. "You've got to believe they'll do the right thing. We have to trust them." He was a hero in World War II and saw violent death up close. He believed in our leaders. Of course in his time the leaders were FDR, Churchill, de Gaulle, Truman, Eisenhower and Kennedy.

January 25 **The Heaven Sent Bard**

Robert Burns, the National Poet of Scotland whose birthday is today, was – in modern terminology – a sex addict. For example, he and a local farm girl were discovered in *flagrante delicto* and hauled before a panel of Presbyters, grim-faced and grimly-bearded elders of the Scottish Presbyterian Kirk.

The couple sat next to each other on stools while for

hours threats, hellfire, brimstone, guilt, sin and eternal damnation rained down upon them. At the start, however, Burns spied the curve of his friend's thigh beneath her skirt and he thought of little else for the entire time.

January 26   **What's Your Fancy?**

Facebook groups frequently cater to highly specialized interests, some kinky even to a sophisticate like me. Consider "Swimming In Our Clothes" (exactly what it says), "The Medieval Christian Tradition" (charming section on The Spanish Inquisition) and my favorite, "Gay Men Who Love Corduroy".

If you're a gay man who surrounds himself with ribbed cotton fabrics, you've found a home. Tomorrow, I launch my own group. It's called Heterosexuals Who Don't Understand Rudimentary Math. If you're straight and hate numbers, I hope you join.

January 27   **Hello Mr Chips**

The Gunnery in Washington, Connecticut, is a posh boarding school for the offspring of the wealthy. Like Choate Rosemary Hall, Kent and Horace Mann, it's an Ivy League "feeder" school and the yearly tuition is equal to the 2019 GDP of Belgium. When circumstances brought me there on a Saturday morning in autumn, the campus gleamed with fall colors, the

architecture was elegantly Palladian and the clouds' scudding seemed choreographed by Baryshnikov.

The library was brimming with lawyers, academics and financiers to be, each in the school's uniform of tie, white V-neck sweater and blue blazer. Every student possessed an eager scholarship I never knew and a net worth beyond imagining.

January 28   

The Diplomatic Red Sash

US foreign policy genius George Kennan designed the policy that ultimately defeated the USSR. Decades ago, he however may have made a stunningly prescient prediction. Kennan warned of what he called the coarsening of America. He predicted ugly, baleful developments for our nation because of anti-intellectualism and xenophobia. He foresaw Trump, Roger Stone, McConnell, the Deplorables, the Proud Boys, the lot. He foresaw the venom, the madness. There can be no comfort in this.

January 29   # Spot?

Over the years, I've met a variety of dogs, cats, two budgies and a goldfish called Oliver. I took note of these pets who share my name. Thus it was when my son was born three-and-a-half decades ago – and this is true – that I urged we name him Rover. My long-suffering (and now ex-) wife, exhausted from the rigors of childbirth, found this line of discussion unedifying. It was one of many of my lines of discussion she rightly found unedifying.

January 30 — **White Goods**

I worked at GE for 20 years and for 20 years, when invited to somebody's home for dinner, I'd get an impassioned lecture about shitty appliances. "I'm but a lowly speechwriter in GE Capital and know nothing of appliances", never proved exculpatory.

Never, not once.

January 31 — **Chef-in-Chief**

This snowy winter afternoon finds me in the warm kitchen at Bellevue House where, apart from doing the washing up, I have no business. Today's an exception. I'm making my signature dish, *Boeuf Carbonnade*, a fabulously rich stew made with buckets of Belgian ale and served over noodles. When I made it for a long ago dinner party, I overdid the sugar for the caramelized onions and the whole thing tasted like meaty Frosted Mini-Wheats. We're hoping for a better outcome today.

February 1 — **Crunch Time**

I'm shown here operating a two-and-a-half tonne vibrating stone crusher in Wales, in a park created at great expense by the City of Newport. It soon became clear, however, the elderly from the nearby care home couldn't visit. The gravel on the footpaths was too large and their wheelchairs wouldn't budge. GE to the rescue. I got the keys to the crusher because, as a speechwriter and not a salesperson, I was expendable.

February 2 — **Button Down**

If I ever get another dog, I'm going to name him Collar. That way, when the mailman came to the door, I'd shout, "Collar, stay!" and he would. If he were a police dog, he'd have a lot of collars. If he ran off, I could say that Collar's loose. Good dog, Collar. Check back frequently for more cerebral humour and trenchant insights.

February 3   The Good News!

As we drove about Connecticut house hunting long ago, my daughter, Mary, noticed a billboard proclaiming Christ Is Risen! It included a depiction of Him and His beating heart surrounded by thorns. Unbidden, she said, "If He's such a big deal, why does He need to advertise?" She was eight.

February 4   Butt One Life to Give

Forty years ago, I went to a Manhattan Holiday Inn to meet with a humorless CIA recruiter called Frank Jeton. (Jeton is French for a gambling chip. Cool right?) Among other things, he said, "Have you ever had a homosexual experience past the age of 17?" Mr Jeton asked this with the seriousness of a 60-year-old man addressing a 29-year-old man in a tatty West Side hotel room. "Oh, no Sir," I responded brightly. "But if it's for my country, I'm willing to learn." I didn't get hired, my school spirit notwithstanding.

February 5   Where's My Jock Strap

A sleek new gym opened near my apartment three years ago. "Have you ever picked up a dumbbell?" the print ad in the window asked coyly. I stopped in to hear their pitch and take a tour. The design and lighting suggested a hip nightclub, not a joint where you jiggle and sweat. You jiggle and sweat in a nightclub too, of course, but I rarely wear white socks and a jock strap to such places.

The manager said the gym was big on amenities, but I thought he said manatees and I spent the rest of the session completely confused. I was of course exhausted by all this walking around looking at stupid exercise stuff. The good news – my fitness goals for the quarter were met, so I immediately celebrated with beer and pizza.

February 6   **Fine Dining**

I often dined in a posh London restaurant that categorized the mains as *Meat – Fish – Crustacea*. I would have gone with exoskeleton, but I'm not a restaurateur.

February 7   **Times that Try Men's Souls**

Revolutionary War propagandist Thomas Paine, whom Teddy Roosevelt called "a filthy little atheist", moved hearts and minds in the run-up to American independence. When it was over, Washington urged him to go help the French with their revolution, which Paine did to little effect.

Revolutionaries are unwelcome once the Revolution is done, what with their incessant pounding on the table upsetting the tea cups and all.

Of the nascent United States, Paine wrote, "We have it in our power to begin the world over again" – an ineffable description of The American Experiment. It's important for us as Americans to remember we still do. We are not exceptional. We're an experiment and a beautiful one too.

February 8 02:12 Hrs

I've put on weight and it may have to do with my eating habits. Earlier this evening, for example, I enjoyed three huge pieces of pepperoni pizza, then a container of ice cream, all washed down with a bottle of *Gevery-Chambertin*. I'm

  now enjoying late night gastrointestinal warfare. I went to see my doctor the other day – he's not a nice man. During the exam, he told me to open my mouth and say, "oink". In parting, he advised me to stay clear of electrified fences.

February 9 A Day of Worship

The sky is dry here in Saratoga, but rain comes down from the trees, their ice melting in warmish air. At 388 Broadway, home of Comedy Works, the faithful of The Next Level Pentecostal Church gather in the basement without a whiff of irony. I leave poetry and piety to others, but sometimes, of a Sunday, Saratoga Springs seems settled and magical.

February 10 Stars and Gripes

I've spent a lifetime studying American history. But it was only a few years ago that I learned of an Italian called Philip Mazzei. A Renaissance man himself – physician, wine-maker, innovative agriculturist, philosopher, writer, arms dealer – Mazzei was Jefferson's Virginia neighbor.

In an impassioned conversation long before the

Revolution, he told the future president that English Common Law needed
improvement, that there was a better
way, that we didn't need a monarch at
all. This moment of insight changed
Thomas Jefferson from a wealthy
landed "Englishman" to a revolutionary
American. Were it not for Mazzei, we
might still be subjects of Her Britannic
Majesty.

February 11   Quadratic Equations My Ass

My personal library contains several books which purport
to show the beauty and art of mathematics. They do not.
In my every math class, after two weeks, I was three weeks
behind. Nasty business math.

February 12   Glitterati

I'm old enough to remember when flying was glamorous.
My first flight was in 1968, New York to Paris and I was
15. At Kennedy, I requested and was served a Manhattan.
Everybody on the plane looked like a movie star, especially
the stewardesses. As was the custom, the flatware was
chilled and the duck was wonderful, once you scraped off
the aspic – glamorous stuff for a distinctly unglamorous
boy. I never thanked my father properly for his largess, but
there was much I never thanked him for.

February 13   This Gets My Goat

In the Roman festival of *Lupercalia*, observed from February 13th to 15th, young men, clothed only in goat-skin loincloths, ran around a track, striking people they passed with a piece of goatskin. This was said to cure infertility. I suggested just such a festival at a recent Saratoga Springs City Council meeting and now the police come to my house three times a week for a wellness check, whatever the hell that is.

February 14   Kiss Up

Today is the feast of St Valentine, the patron saint of love, bee-keeping and fainting. Just go tell dishy Janice in Accounts Receivable how you feel about her, then have some honey and then swoon. Maybe she'll revive you. How effin hot would that be?

February 15   Friends Like These

In our youth at *soirées* various, my friend, Captain Michael Lodington Soares, USN (Ret), and I bantered wittily, enjoyed adult beverages, crawled up the curtains, scared the virgins, then left on our hands and knees. A *belle époque* really, unless you were a curtain. During our 50-year friendship, we didn't talk every day, we usually talked twice a day. As my then-wife memorably put it, "I don't like it when he's around. I can't control you". For five years, Michael got more laughs out of brain cancer than you'd think possible, but one December day in 2019 the laughter stopped.

February 16   **Pretty in Red**

In 1990, a friend and I went to see a magnificent play in London's West End called **Jeffrey Barnard Is Unwell**. It starred Peter O'Toole. In the seat to my right was Molly Ringwald and to her right her date, actor Peter Weller (RoboCop, Naked Lunch, Sons of Anarchy). Funnily enough, Mr Weller and I shared the same flight from New York. The play was brilliant and hilarious and O'Toole was in great form. The Apollo Theatre (and probably much of Shaftesbury Avenue) rocked with laughter.

Nevertheless, Ms Ringwald fell fast asleep during the third act, perhaps from jet lag. She was, still, when awake, a perfectly pleasant neighbour. No armchair dominance, no unnecessary leans, no sleep-induced drool, no disruptive snores. Her birthday is today.

February 17   **Generous Enormous**

I loved being a propagandist for GE Capital, which I was for 18 years. In the 1990s, we bought European and Asian banks like you change your knickers. After three gleaming corporate jets landed, one after another, at a sleepy mid-size [insert country name here] airport, a parade of limos motored to the bank's headquarters. Hot and cold running MBAs, Brits and Americans, descended on the place for two days of due diligence. The return to the airport was every bit as showy.

Back in London, I'd get a call from a furious GE Capital finorkin and the veins in his forehead were throbbing. "How the hell did this story about the Swiss due diligence get into *Les Echoes*?" he'd demand. For operational security, every acquisition had a secret project name. The effort to buy Budapest Bank, for example, was called Project Danube. John le Carré we were not.

February 18 — Spirits in the Material World

This is a photograph of Nellie Jacobs Oliver, my grandmother, who died in the second wave of the Influenza Pandemic of 1918-1919. Her family came to North America from Holland in the early 1700s. My grandfather and her husband, John MacGowan Oliver, kept a notebook in which he recorded every penny he ever made. He also mentioned big events in his life, but always laconically. On 5th July, 1919, he wrote, "Nellie sick". Four days later, "Nellie Died".

February 19 — Police Action

Today, at 2 am, whilst rereading **À la Recherche du Temps Perdu** in the original Greek, intense flashing lights heralded the arrival of Saratoga Springs SWAT at my apartment building. The cops – kitted out with helmets, Kevlar and enough firepower to invade Liechtenstein – saw my massive upper body strength, gimlet eye, ascot, silk smoking jacket, Cuban cigar and opera slippers and instantly asked for help.

The details of our joint investigation are confidential, but I comported myself as you'd expect of a moderately obese English major from a third-rate and now defunct liberal arts college in northwest Jasper County, Indiana. "Why are you wearing opera slippers?" one cop demanded. "I was walking on an aria rug," I replied.

"You need to return to your apartment, Sir. You seem pretty inebriated," barked another cop. "Glad I could help, Your Honour," I said brightly. The Incident Report claims I "squealed girlishly in fear" but this was just acid reflux which afflicts millions of older adults especially after a big dinner. Rest easy America. JPV Oliver is on the watch.

February 20 — **Yummy Gummies**

I've visited the Haribo Shop and Museum in *Uzes*, Provence, France – *Musèe du Bonbon Haribo*. Top that, Poser.

February 21   Beat It, Just Beat It

I knew the drum major for a competitive marching band here in upstate New York. Think light blue coatees, fuzzy red plumes on their tar buckets and an honor guard holding blocks of wood painted white and shaped like rifles. He died in middle age and the entire band, including mildly obese flag twirlers in sequins, attended his funeral, marching purposefully about a church parking lot after mass.

This occurred in a down-at-the-heels river town, where tiny houses smell of cigarettes and heartbreak. Buglers played taps dolefully, as if he'd been killed in combat. In life, he was a hairdresser. His mother, his wife, his ex-wife, his girlfriend and his many children were, if I'm being honest, a little relieved. He'd been a handful.

February 22   Eggs, Fancy

It'd be *infra dig* to bleat about the cost of my breakfast today at a posh Saratoga hotel which I won't name, The Adelphi. The bill was equal to the 2018 GDP of Belgium, but the bacon and mimosas were really good and the hipster guest at the next table sported a Rolex the size of Saturn. Our hipster waiter had not one, but two man buns. Classy.

February 23

Salute Smartly, Charge Up the Hill

German military officer Baron von Steuben, who joined the Continental Army on this day in 1778, is considered a Founding Father of the United States Army. The order, tactics and discipline he brought to the Americans were pivotal in the outcome of the Revolution.

It's likely von Steuben was gay. Records are scant, but his relationships, his career struggles and his bequests to the young men he legally adopted are highly suggestive. This means he's a source of pride for gay people in the US and in Germany – and for gay people in their respective militaries.

February 24

Goosed

Icelandic goose hunters have discovered a 1,000-year-old sword just lying* on the ground in the town of Skaftarhreppur, a word which I'd like you to use in a sentence with coworkers today. The amazing thing about this news is there are wild goose hunters in Iceland.

* Lay Versus Lie

I'd rather discuss the difference between whole- and term-life insurance with a coked-up 29-year-old insurance agent who's panicking because his quarterly sales numbers are due tomorrow. Some people care about the distinction – typically people who use The Vile Oxford Comma – while others think it pedantic twaddle. Next week, we'll address the which/that conundrum, followed by an hour-long video on intransitive verbs.

February 25   Let Me Know When You Start

I just motored to an OR for minor surgery to attack a narrowing of the lower spine. My grasp of medical terms is vast, so I confidently told the nurse I was to have an episiotomy.

> Nurse [condescendingly]: "That's *not* why you're here, Sir."
> Me: "Well, ok, an epistemological, er, an epididymus then. Or something with the Labia. It's in that general region."

The procedure was over in five minutes and I now have the lumbar of an 18-year-old. I've endured more uncomfortable pedicures.

February 26   Taking Flight

Angel wing and vertebrae of a Sunday afternoon in Saratoga Springs.

February 27   Knickers Auld

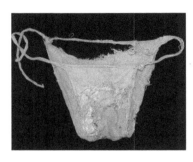

A pair of tatty men's underwear, circa 1500, were discovered in an ancient Austrian castle. They are labeled "Walmart SuperCenter, Graz. Medium."

February 28   Does this Skirt Make Me Look Fat?

Some scholars claim the US isn't a melting pot at all, but more like a salad bowl where ethnic groups maintain powerful connection with the old country (Italian Americans, Irish Americans, Korean Americans, Polish Americans and the like).

OK, if America's a salad bowl, then where's one of its largest immigrant groups, my crowd, the Scots? Highland games aside, we're not big on parades, "Kiss Me I'm Scottish" t-shirts, Saltire face painting and saints' days (sorry Andrew). While glorious, single malts don't count. So what's the Scottish-American food metaphor? Well, we're a steaming plate of finnan haddie that's served after your salad.

March 1   Equality

A reader took exception to my rendering of a famous hotel's name – she regarded the equal sign as a mistake. I plead not guilty. The Waldorf=Astoria Hotel is a compromise between the Waldorfs and the Astors, allowing each to get top billing. And you think your relatives are nuts.

March 2   **ᵁpward!**

I once encountered former NY Governor Hugh Carey in the Bull and Bear Lounge at The Waldorf=Astoria. I nattered on about working in the Legislative Bill Drafting Commission in the Capitol. He was patient, larger than life and a _terrific_ governor – a politician in the best sense of the word. Carey once walked into a press briefing with his hair dyed a shade of auburn unknown in nature. A reporter shouted, "Your hair looks great, Governor!" Carey paused, ran a hand over his tresses and said, "The sap...is _rising_".

March 3   **ᴳun ᴾoint**

Today's the birthday of Olympian Jackie Joyner-Kersee, who nearly got me shot. As part of a PR program I created for my employer, Seagram, I booked her on The Today Show, then broadcasting from Seoul. At the NBC reception desk, we were asked to show our passports but Jackie had left hers at the hotel.

Koreans can be a strict people, with absolute adherence to The Rules. When a senior Today Show producer turned up to bid us entry, a uniformed Seoul police officer pulled his weapon and pointed it at yours truly. Once he was becalmed, we proceeded to the studio unmolested. Jane Pauley is wonderful by the way.

March 4   Time After Time

Of an evening, I came close to time travel at a London gentlemen's club called Buck's; it's in the mold of Whites or Boodles. At the door, a faithful retainer took my coat, a job he'd held for 92 years, and commented on the weather, as is stipulated in The Magna Carta. The interior is dim candlelight, dark paneling and Dickens. After drinks in the lounge, an 80-year-old waitress brought soup to our table, spilling most en route. When we'd consumed the mains and two bottles of claret, she rolled up with a trolley bearing a vast wheel of Stilton.

> Me: "Gosh, I could never eat all that."
> Waitress [in a Cockney accent]: "Oh, you're not meant to eat it all, Sir."
> Me [in British English]: "Quite."

An ocean of Port accompanied the luxurious cheese. Before retiring that night, I beamed back to the 21st Century, but it wasn't easy to leave.

March 5   Let's Rock!

At 13, I was in a rock and roll band. We'd get invited to tween parties and play our set list of two songs over and over (Satisfaction and Gloria). The Beatles we were not and nobody seemed to mind.

March 6   What a Pissoir

JC Decaux, who died at 78 in 2016, was a French designer, advertising genius and entrepreneur. He's famous for his

distinctive street furniture – bus stop enclosures, benches, kiosks, toilets – which can be seen in cities round the world. My employer, GE Capital, considered investing in a JC Decaux scheme for New York City and I was dispatched to the company's sprawling headquarters in a vasty field at *Neuilly-sur-Seine* outside of Paris. With its artificial streets and abundant cityscapes, the place is redolent of a Hollywood movie lot. Unforgettable really, as was M Decaux.

March 7 **Side Car, G&T, Rob Roy!**

The Oxford English Dictionary or OED is one of humankind's great accomplishments and the story of its creation is a triumph of 19th Century scholarship. Sadly, The OED missed by a mile today with the word highball, an evening ritual for millions of Americans from the 1930s to the 1970s. OED ignored that sense of the word in favor of a railroad meaning. Life goes on, but I'm starting this Saturday evening with a, well, you know.

March 8 **That's Novel**

My next book is called **The Grapenuts of Wrath**, a gripping tale of family, redemption, love, grinding poverty and the importance of a complete breakfast. Look for it wherever books or cereal are sold.

March 9 **Another Rye and Ginger?**

This witty bit of business hung at the entrance to the bar in the cellar of The Pink Palace, the Oliver ancestral manse.

March 10 **English Wit**

"If at first you don't succeed, failure may be your style" and "Persistence is crucial. It is in the nature of barriers that they fall".

> – Quentin Crisp, English bureaucrat, raconteur and author
> (**The Naked Civil Servant**), whom I ran into in front of my
> Manhattan apartment building in 1981. We chatted for
> three quarters of an hour and he was delightful.

March 11 **Pi in the Sky**

There's much in American politics to make the blood run cold, however I have discovered something worse. The Weizmann Institute of Science near Tel Aviv is offering a course in recreational math. I'm sure you're as sickened by this as I am. Math is the greatest scourge to ever befall the human race – greater than war, pestilence, disease or

Mitch McConnell. Math is the ill-behaved feces-flinging snot-nosed oppositional-defiant stepchild of Science.

I just called The Institute to register my profound objection to "recreational math". It's after midnight in Tel Aviv and I spoke to a nice security guard named Ben, who, when I told him, was affronted too. However with the faculty and staff asleep, his hands are tied. The guard said, "We Jews love learning, but there's just no excuse for this." Right on, Ben. If you wish to register your outrage, Ben's on duty till 9 pm, US Eastern Standard Time. The Weismann Institute's number from the US is 011-972-8-934-9106. Let's stop the madness.

March 12 **From Sea to Shining Sea**

The Founders would recognize the divided and angry American Republic. Washington complained of the Continental Army's soldiers who spoke back to officers, refused direct orders and were big on debating. Jefferson believed Hamilton schemed for a return to British rule (he did not). The agrarian South always mistrusted the money center and industrial North.

Shay's Rebellion, the Whiskey Rebellion, Jim Crow laws, the KKK, States' Rights, the Three Fifths Compromise and the Civil War are emblematic of a people who believe themselves ill-treated by government. Seems independent-minded settlers who really didn't like Europe weren't so thrilled with America either. They still aren't.

March 13   My Favourite Hates

A pal asks what my principle dislikes are. Here's The Top Ten.

10. Wax Beans
9. Wind Chimes
8. Cats
7. Dental Dams
6. Nose Hair
5. **"Gilmore Girls"**
4. **"The Blind Side"**
3. Hardware Stores
2. Broadway Musicals
1. **"The Blind Side"**

"The Blind Side" gets two mentions because it's that awful.

March 14   Man of the House

In the center is John MacGowan Oliver, my Scots-Canadian grandfather. A conductor on the New York Central Railroad, he and his coworkers are shown sitting on the cowcatcher of an ancient locomotive. JMacGO had a troubled mind. In 1911, he was institutionalized after a psychotic break and, for much of his adult life, he believed the 50 or so patent medicines on his dresser were the only things keeping him alive.

March 15   **Pass the Paprika**

Today in America it's National Hungarian Day. Circa 1996, my employer, GE Capital, bought a big retail bank headquartered in Budapest. Parliament, opposition parties and the press objected to the terms of the deal, so I worked on crisis management with Lajos Bokros, the nation's finance minister who'd negotiated the deal on their side. The bank was kaput, but Hungarians still believed we Capitalists were somehow stealing the crown jewels.

The bank's president, a senior officer in the Hungarian intelligence service, believed GE Capital and the USA were executing a secret plan for world domination. In a secure room in the bank's headquarters, I reminded him the institution was broke. Domestic media coverage was melodramatic, the prose often purple. Describing my propaganda, a Budapest newspaper wrote, *"Pity the wolf who howls that his paws are bloodied by the lamb's raw flesh"*.

March 16   **Nature Walk**

In the forest, if I'm confronted by a bear, I plan to play dead. This will be good practice for when the bear kills me.

March 17   **More Blue Beer for My Friends**

Maewyn Succat's feast day falls today. You may know him as St Patrick, but that wasn't his name at birth. He was probably born in Scotland to Roman parents. In iconography, Mr Succat was portrayed wearing blue vestments, but Irish marketers changed it to green early in the 20th Century. *Begora.*

March 18   **The Wisdom of Spring**

At 67, one confronts certain hard realities. I'll never speak fluent French. No six pack abs. I won't understand Wittgenstein. I don't like snails. Death before bunions. Fuck bunions man. Funyuns – different story.

Oh, but I did get the girl of my dreams. Happy spring.

March 19   **Celebration**

Today is the birthday of Dr David Livingstone (1813 – 1873), African explorer and anti-slavery activist. Fact: his actual surname was "*Livingstone I Presume*". To honour the occasion, I present my *tableau vivant extraordinaire*, in which I rock a pith helmet.

March 20   **Get Out**

For 10 years, my little brood and I lived in Philipse Manor, Sleepy Hollow, NY, a few miles from *Kykuit*, the Rockefeller estate at Pocantico Hills with its commanding views of the Hudson River. Our next-door neighbor was the only secretary in the Rockefellers' office there and had been for as long as anybody could remember. One afternoon David – who died on this date in 2017 – popped in to say they were letting her go for budget reasons.

"Imagine being told by a Rockefeller they can't afford you," she noted with asperity.

March 21   **Jamesian**

"Therefore I say unto you, take no thought for your life, what ye shall eat, what ye shall drink; nor yet for your body, nor what ye shall put on. Is not the life more than meat, the body than raiment?"

– Matthew 6:25, **The King James Bible**

March 22   **Canterbury, England, Circa 1978**

John Gavins, me and Zerihun Tessema.

John "Gavo" Gavins now heads an Australian accountancy firm and Zerihun Tessema (R), an Ethiopian, was an academic in London until his death in 2018. In 1978, having left the Ethiopian Ministry of Finance, Zeri followed the vicious armed conflict in Eritrea relentlessly from Canterbury, where we were in grad school.

He'd exult or be grimly silent depending on the headlines each day. Decades later, I was dining alone in a London pub when I was approached by what I thought was a stranger. It was Zeri. Later that night, we drunkenly tried calling Gavo in Australia and, happily for my phone bill, failed. In 2021, there's a vicious war in Eritrea again.

March 23   **First Name: Eleanor**

Mrs Carter seemed so fragile when we met in the White House's Diplomatic Reception Room, I wondered how she sustained life. Well, she continues to do a jolly good job at 93. That day I was off keeping a low profile in the corner with the Secret Service guy. She was having none of it.

March 24   𝔗hat's the 𝔓lan

In anticipation of a less frat boy existence, and to demonstrate my sophistication, I just installed a shower curtain that doubles as a map of the world.

Manufacturer Saturday Knight Ltd helpfully notes, "This curtain is intended for decorative purposes only and does not conform *exactly* to Global Map Accuracy Standards". [Emphasis mine.]

The Saturday Knight staff really know their way around sophisticated word play and they sometimes use their products for transoceanic navigation. Whilst showering, and with a guest or two in the *salle de bain*, I sure appreciate the strategic location of Tierra del Fuego.

March 25   𝔓op! 𝔉izz!

When *Dom Pérignon* (1638 - 1715) discovered the bubbly French wine for which he is justifiably famous, he most certainly did not say, *"Alors ! I am dreen keen zee STAIRS!"* That iconic phase was actually coined for a 19th Century Paris ad campaign.

I mention the Dom because shops in the City of Saratoga Springs,

NY – supposedly an *au courant* berg – do not offer ice buckets and crystal Champagne flutes. I'm sure you're as repulsed by this as I am. I call upon the town's merchants to correct this indefensible condition with immediate effect or accept the consequences.

March 26   And a Sexy Librarian

Plans were announced today for The Donald J Trump Presidential Library, to be located at The Aqueduct Race Track and Casino in Queens, NY. The Library will house all 15 books written by Mr Trump. Many will be first editions so scholars can study the best commercial real estate deals in Queens and how to date Eastern European models. "This is a classy race track and my books are classy books," the ex-president said.

"The Trump Library will have three great snack bars, with cold draft beer, nachos and a Hooters with the hottest broads you ever saw. You can spend a day betting on the best ponies – the very best ponies – then hit The Presidential Gift Shop for, you know, coasters, CDs, Melania Dish Towels and autographed pictures of me being president," the disgraced ex-president added.

Former White House Spokesman Sean Spicer is developing a Las Vegas-style nightclub show for the Trump Hooters, sources said, and Wednesday and Thursday will be Ladies' Nites. The Trump Presidential Library was going to be located on Rikers Island, Queens, but developers couldn't overcome objections from inmates and guards at New York City's most notorious prison.

March 27   **Blue Collar Blues**

The following exchange just took place between two electricians.

> Worker Guy 1: "Hey Tommy! What's up?"
> Worker Guy 2: "My fuckin' blood pressure, my fuckin' cholesterol, my fuckin' debt and my fuckin' mother-in-law's up from Queens".
> Worker Guy 1: "Shit, Tommy. That sucks".

March 28   **A Nonce**

A review in The NYTs book section described a dead squid hanging in a museum.

"It's poor legs limp, spaghettical." Please use the word in a sentence today. For example, say to your wife, "Gosh, Sarah, in all this humidity, your hair looks really spaghettical." Oh how she'll laugh and laugh.

March 29   **A Beautiful Mind**

Often at Seagram, we dined "downstairs", at the storied Four Seasons restaurant and my stratospheric expense

reports went unchallenged. In The Grill Room, where one routinely sat near The Great and The Good and thought nothing of it, celebrity was regarded with *sang-froid*. There was for me, and doubtless others, an exception.

One day, Abba Eban, the Israeli Foreign Minister, was in the booth just across the way. He had, that morning, addressed the UN General Assembly. Eban was one of the brilliant minds and great diplomats of the 20th Century. The Four Seasons Restaurant, which opened in 1959 and long ago moved out of The Seagram Building, went out of business in 2018.

March 30   How to Write

Social media posts are a vibrant literary form, each one having a potential audience in the billions. Writing posts requires creativity, insight and deep soul-searching. Such epigrams sometimes achieve the profound. That's why I always start a writing session with some Miller Lites and a can of Pringles.

March 31   The Battle of Saratoga

I here discuss the pivotal Battle of Saratoga and its lasting impact. So what happened was this. In 1997, Gina Malottzi, who assistant-managed The Finish Line Salon on Broadway, battled her roofer husband, Jimmy Kowtowski, in a big divorce that went on for almost two weeks. Jimmy had partied with some local gals one night because it was

Daniella Hennessey's birthday and they were real tight in high school and one thing led to another as sometimes happens. When she found out, Gina, a good Catholic, landed a cast iron skillet on Jimmy's noggin so hard he spent nine days in Saratoga Hospital.

The roofing business went kablooey and Jimmy had to sell his Ford F-450 Super Duty pickup truck, which he effin loved, and his brother and business partner, Tommy, went bankrupt and started doing meth. Both guys made good money up to then. The families shoot daggers at each other at church and in the liquor store even after all this time. In court, Jimmy actually called Gina "a wacky ballerina", which is really not cool, given her dad's temper and all.

April 1   **Peep Show**

Easter is a big day for Christians around world, because it's on that day they are reminded the deity is like a perfectly crafted, but elusive, French *soufflé*.

He is risen.

April 2   **Big BD!**

Charlemagne, born on this date in 748, championed learning and Christianity, united Western and Central Europe, ruled the Holy Roman Empire and brought order to a disordered Europe. But just last week, scholars made surprising discoveries about his life.

Circa 769, when he was King of the Franks, Charlemagne refined the ancient Frankish sport of Frisbee Golf ("Le Golffe de Frisbeeshe") and, on a trip to visit the Lombards, he invented Beer Pong. After his death, Charlemagne's oldest son, Pepin the Hunchback, claimed his father came

up with the idea for Scrabble, but there is no historical evidence to support this and I think Pepin was just getting too far out over his skis.

It's a rookie mistake to confuse Pepin the Hunchback with Pepin the Short, who preceded Charlemagne as Holy Roman Emperor and, let's face it, you're no rookie.

He's shown looking regal and dodgy.

April 3   # 𝔍o Begin and Cease

Of the several ways of beginning a book which are now in practice in the known world, I am confident my own way of doing it is the best – I'm sure it is the most religious – for I begin with writing the first sentence – and trusting to Almighty God for the second.

—**The Life and Opinions of Tristram Shandy, Gentleman**,
by Laurence Sterne, 1759.

April 4   # My Therapist

MT: "John, you're a good person with some challenging ideation."
Me: "The word ideation is an insult to educated people everywhere."
MT: "Okay, we're done for this week. Next Tuesday at 7?"
Me: "Sure. I'll bring better ideations."

Ours was a fraught therapeutic relationship.

April 5 — **Cuisine Shakespearean**

Combine brown sugar, paprika, cumin, mustard, garlic powder, onion powder, cayenne, salt and chili powder in a bowl and then use your hands to spread that concoction over the meat. Aye, there's the rub.

April 6 — **Antler Clicking**

I once bragged to a GE coworker about having fired an M-16, a .44 Magnum, a Glock, etc, at a California gun range. He said, "When I was a Congressional aide, they took me to Quantico where I fired a TOW missile and blew up a tank" – quite the conversation stopper that.

April 7 — **Ringside**

A boss once gave me two front row tickets for boxing matches at New York's famed Madison Square Garden.

"These are press passes and obviously you're not press," he warned. "So make up a good story and don't do anything stupid."

I instantly forgot his admonition and a pal and I headed for 7th Avenue.

At the MSG gate, the ticket-taker wanted to know what newspaper we represented. Without thinking, I said, "Oh I'm the assistant sports editor at The Wall Street Journal and this guy's the photo editor." Never mind I had no pen and notepad and never mind my friend had no camera and never mind that, in those days, The WSJ didn't run pictures and had no sports page. He waved us in.

The draw that night was famous African boxer Azuma Nelson from Ghana. When Nelson began to pummel his opponent, which he did immediately, Azuma's fans beat their war drums ominously. The effect was dazzling.

April 8   ## The Tail of the Curious Bunny

This wee rabbit, whom I call Lodington, inhabits the back garden at Bellevue House, Saratoga. He's as full of questions as a five-year-old and he loves to watch me prepare the grill for a charcoaly feast, as I'm doing now. He's a bit of a ham really and stayed stock still while I took his picture. Then he demanded a picture from a different angle. Lodington was at pains this evening to wish everybody a happy spring. He's one big-hearted bunny.

April 9   ## The Age of Reason

My peregrinations now in abeyance, I am enveloped by the warm spring of the English countryside, as glorious a security blanket as ever devised by Mother Nature, and, here in the garden of a great country house, I am reminded of my hero, Lord Berners. He once wanted to avoid a dull couple lunching at his country home, so he fobbed them off on his catamite.

LB soon realised however he needed a book from the library – where lunch was being served. He covered himself with a hearthrug, crawled into the library on his hands and knees, extended a hand from beneath the rug, grabbed the book in question and crawled out. This puzzled the guests. Later, when asked why he did such a thing, Lord Berners said in his characteristic stutter, "I didn't want to make a spec, spec, spectacle of myself".

April 10 — **Health, History and Horses**

Saratoga Springs, NY, has a famous thoroughbred racetrack, circa 1863, Victorian mansions, numberless pubs and restaurants, swank shops, nine museums and an upmarket college. But it also includes the 1970 Stonequist Apartments – public housing for the poor, diminished and disabled. I'm a student of architecture and I call this building The Soviet Excrescence. One hundred Stonequist windows face South Federal Street and, of those, four still have brave Christmas lights that twinkle in the warm spring night.

April 11 — **Magyar Moola**

In Hungary, the basic monetary unit is the *Forint*, known internationally as the HUF. As I write, there's HUF308.919

to US$1.00. *Forint* is redolent of the Renaissance city-state of Florence, which started issuing gold coins in 1252. The economy was so stable, so respected, their money was the regional standard for trade. In linguistics, *forint* is a wanderword.

April 12   **Psalm 119: 157**

Consider how I love Thy precepts: quicken me, O LORD, according to Thy loving kindness. Except for Thy holy global murderous plague, O LORD, which was kind of shitty of Thou if I'm being totally honest. O LORD, Thou worketh in mysterious ways, but sometimes Thou can be a little Dickish. Many are my persecutors and mine enemies, but Thou need not smite me and sprinkle holy water on them. I mean, really, O LORD, give it a rest. I'm on my last nerve over here.

April 13   **Busted**

I've been mocked for using utensils to eat my hamburger or slice of pizza.

Presented herewith a photo of then British PM David Cameron at a 4th of July event in America some years ago. I struggle with what cufflinks to wear for such events. Of the English, humourist SJ Perelman said, "There's such a thing as too much couth".

April 14 — Buh Buy

I rise to give full-throated support to "died", "death" and "dead" versus "passing", "passed" and "pass."

The public are urged to reserve the latter group for Walmart and kidney stones. Usage examples:

"Todd, you oaf, you just passed the Walmarts."

Or

"When you pass that kidney stone, Gwen, I hope you shut your pie hole for two seconds."

When I die, if you say, "John passed", I'll haunt you for eternity.

April 15 — CPAs on Parade

It's likely the first name recorded in writing belonged to a Sumerian administrator circa 3,400 BCE. Tellingly, he was not a beloved poet, a powerful king or a great philosopher. He was an accountant named *Kushim*. Happy tax day.

April 16 — Da!

The USSR produced a genre of political jokes. Here's one.

In a rural area outside Moscow, where a crushing drought had lasted for six months, Comrade Agriculture Commissar decided to visit a local farmer.

Comrade Agriculture Commissar: Comrade Farmer, how is your potato crop this year?

Comrade Farmer: I will tell you, Comrade Commissar. If you piled up all my potatoes, they'd reach to God's knees.

CAC: But, Comrade Farmer, we know there is no God.

CF: That is true, Comrade Commissar. And we also know there are no potatoes.

April 17 **Interior Decoration**

Charlie King and Anna MacSwan recently bought a lovely new home in London's Sydenham neighbourhood. Like most new homeowners, they were over the moon and began extensive renovations, including steaming off the tired wallpaper that adorned the master bedroom for over 50 years.

A surprising and long-hidden message was revealed, however, when Charlie did the room's back wall. There in all-caps was the sentence, "DEREK HAS GOT A BIG PRICK". Charlie and Anna haven't located Derek just yet, but as you can see from their eager young faces, they're not giving up.

April 18   **Stalled**

I'm sitting on a toilet in the men's room of The Saratoga Casino Hotel. A gravelly-voiced woman just flung the main door open and shouted something.

She either said, *"ANYBODY IN HERE? I GOTTA MOP!"* or *"THE BUILDING'S ON FIRE. RUN FOR YOUR LIFE."* More as it becomes available.

April 19   **Beep, Beep, Um, Beep, Beep**

My father bought a new Cadillac nearly every year of his adult life. I once saw him round the corner on Osborne Road with the latest version and I, a little boy, actually thought he'd brought home the Batmobile. His belief in what was then a crappy, but stylish, ride was unshakable. The fins on his cars were gloriously aeronautical.

Car-from-UK.com

April 20   **Of Thee I Sing**

Americans began changing the fork from one hand to the other circa 1820. Because it was different than the English practice, it was regarded as patriotic. Only a few years after The Revolution and The War of 1812, such symbolism mattered.

April 21   **One Night in London**

While at university, a girlfriend and I went to the theatre in the West End and another couple joined. The play, about American politics, was unspeakably bad – clumsy American accents and actors so wooden they could have been polished with Mr Sheen Multi-Surface Spray Wax. At the interval, when we snuck out a side door, things instantly turned awkward.

The door opened into a stunningly posh private gaming club – millionaires in dinner suits and cocktail dresses illuminated by 100-year-old crystal chandeliers. The clattering arrival of four bewildered, tatty and penniless grad students into the bright light brought the glittering casino to an immediate halt. We made a beeline for the nearest exit and, once outside, bumped right into a gigantic Rolls Royce blocking the footpath.

Inexplicably, the car's owner asked where we were headed and bade the chauffeur open the doors for us. During the ride, we conversed wittily, including the driver. The rich aroma of that car's interior made up for the play.

April 22   **Our Changing Bodies**

Even absent serious physical or mental illness, our bodies still present challenges as we age. Here are three from my own experience and, as a man who has devoted his life to science, you can trust my comments completely.

- The sciatic nerve is the oppositional-defiant lamebrain oaf of the human form. A loudmouthed Trump supporter, it believes in conspiracy theories and refuses to wear a facemask at the supermarket because the Libtards made the whole goddamn thing up to get that effin Commie Biden elected. The sciatic nerve's angry about his poor life-choices and his shitty job at the plant. His favorite expression is, "This is bullshit, man".
- Everybody's run into that salesman who won't leave you alone. You say, "I'm just looking" and still he follows you around like a mental patient in the Subaru dealership, Best Buy or Jos A Banks. That in a nutshell is the prostate. It's overweight, loves the New England Patriots, has a man-crush on Tom Brady and thinks Busch Light is good beer. I know this because next Thursday I'm having a procedure to address my issues "down there". My fiancée calls this a prostate facelift, but I don't think that's funny.
- Highly educated and pedantic, the arthritic lower spine is both a tortured intellectual and All But Dissertation. He corrects everybody's grammar at cocktail parties and regards himself as funny which he is resolutely not. The lower spine speaks four languages and is always quoting The London Review of Books right to your face. The only thing that shuts him up is the intervention of his wife, Abigale "Gabby" Penton.

In what ways is your body changing?

April 23   St George's Day

I love the English. From them America got its language, legal system, the separation of church and state, the social contract, Churchill, best friend in the world and much else besides. I went to graduate school there for about 10, maybe 15 minutes. For work, I spent more time in London than in New York. The English gave me numberless personal kindnesses over the years and I got an English hatter, haberdasher, shirt maker, bespoke tailor and Bath Oliver biscuits too. Also, their gin is great.

But if we're being honest, they heat their bath towels, but not their rooms. A hot water bottle warms a postage stamp bit of the bed. They've got a special device that makes toast cold. Bed tea is creepy when brought to your darkened room at 5 am by your hirsute host in knickers that have seen better days. By law, the English aren't allowed to make new friends past the age of 11. They never shut up about Brexit.

When they move to North America, they persist in saying car park, bonnet, lift, petrol and other arcane Medieval words. Anyway, happy St George's Day to their patron saint, who was born in what is now Turkey, was a soldier not a knight and who never set foot in England.

April 24   Le Grande Fromage

Throughout the rolling year, we each have occasions especially dear to us – a birthday, anniversary, a holiday or The International Granite Workers Festival.

On my favorite occasion, National Cheese Day, which falls today, many wonderful fermented curds come to mind – *Comté*, *St Albray*, Extra-Aged Cheddar, Double Gloucester and *Appenzeller*, for instance.

But there can only be one King and that, Lords, Ladies and Gentlemen, is Stilton. A wheel of that and a bottle of Port and the banter flows like a mountain stream in spring. If you don't agree, I hope you get a pimple on your tongue as you force the last squirt from an expired can of Cheez Whiz onto a soppy Ritz cracker.

April 25   𝔓oesy

Of a long ago summer night, my daughter, Mary, came to visit to my apartment in Sandy Hook, Connecticut. She arrived direct from the farmers' market with pesto from Norwalk and proper mozzarella from New Britain and fresh bread and tomatoes and sweet snap peas and kindness. Before she made sandwiches, she handed me a book.

"What am I looking for?" I asked.

"Just keep going till you find a poem," she said.

Good advice that. Mary, an educator who specializes in wilderness educational programs, can differentiate between five kinds of bear poop. Cheers to my Best Baby, pictured in Hawaii when she was teaching there.

April 26 — **Light the Lights!**

Lin-Manuel Miranda, the writer of **Hamilton**, announced today he's bringing a new musical to Broadway. It's a ribald imagining of Sen Lindsay Graham's private life. It might be called **Taint Misbehavin'!** or **The Perineum Monologues**, but, either way, it's sure to be a monster hit.

April 27 — **The Raj**

My guide during a couple of trips to India, the owner of a big PR consultancy, was a highly educated, informed and cheerful fellow. Except once. On the way to a soirée, he listened attentively as I described my protocol visit to the Ministry of Finance earlier in the day.

We joked about bureaucrats, American and Indian. The Ministry building is an architectural marvel built of sandstone by the English during the Raj and I said how much I admired the edifice. There was a sudden conversational lull, the only one I had with him. After a long pause, he looked out the car's window and whispered, "God, I hated them". He wasn't talking to me.

April 28 — **Ars Longa, Vita Brevis**

The Picasso tapestry, called *Le Tricorne*, hung in the lobby of The Seagram Building where I toiled for 10 years. I'd stroll by it most days on the way to The Four Seasons for boozy lunches. We referred to the iconic restaurant, where Manhattan publishers, writers, celebrities and power brokers dined, as "downstairs".

One frequently bumped into a small, elegantly turned-out older man with big round spectacles – renowned architect Philip Cortelyou Johnson who helped design the very skyscraper in which we worked and ate.

April 29   # ℞eduction in ℱorce

After breakfasting on kippers, a rasher of bacon and Champagne, I summoned my trusted valet, chauffeur and batman, Finial, to the library. He well knew I was making him redundant and he took it like the dignified sapper he was for so many years. Stout fellow, Finial. He's been at my side since the Suez, so today's was a grim task, but I hope for his return when The Plague clears.

I regret to say his wife, Margaret Mary Siobhan, wasn't so stoic. At one point, she threatened me by brandishing a hot curling iron. I put this down to the cooking sherry she'd quaffed since dawn. Emotive people, the Irish. Finial is shown, in the Crimea, in happier days.

April 30   # Our Friend in Science

WARNING: EXPLICIT LANGUAGE. DISCRETION IS ADVISED.

This is important health information for men of a certain age and those who love them. As a man of science, you can trust my advice utterly. Yesterday, I underwent a complex surgical procedure called a Urolift or "Prostate Facelift". Here's what happens.

A highly trained surgeon gently inserts a Louisville Slugger (in other nations, a Kookaburra Kahuna brand cricket bat is used) fitted with a large video camera into the urethra. It's threaded deep into the bladder and the adjacent tibia and clavicle in search of *Perigord* black truffles (*Tuber Melanosporum*). Normally, this is done in early spring in northern climes when the delicious and vastly expensive mushrooms flourish.

When extracted, the truffles, packed in dry ice, are sent via a Gulfstream V to NYC for distribution to five star restaurants around the world. The surgeon then calls the patient's emergency contact to say how well he, the patient, did whilst completely unconscious.

The patient is then instructed to pee like a racehorse, which feels exactly like someone in 1761 in the throws of tertiary gonorrhea.

Contact me directly if you have specific questions. I've already said too much.

May 1   **Smooth Operator**

The May issue of Esquire magazine helpfully provides a list of the best songs to have on the Victrola whilst one is engaged in the act of sexual congress. For the most part, it's composed of singers I've never heard of, suggesting I should never canoodle again. Well, I'll tell you what, Esquire, I don't want some multimillionaire South American warbler caterwauling away whilst I'm trying to have it off. I have enough trouble as it is. AND, what if the record skips?

May 2   𝕷ove, Medieval Style

Heloise and Abelard were the greatest love story of the Middle Ages. They had drama, forbidden romance, intensity, God, heartbreak, aching sadness, castration, brimstone and smutty sex in a field. They also had a child out of wedlock whom they named Astrolabe after an ancient device mariners used to determine the position of their ships.

The nice people at the OED have astrolabe as the word of the day, but – unforgivably – they make no mention of H, A or their offspring. In *l'Ecole Militaire*, when an idiotic order was barked on the walkie-talkie, which was often, a common reply was, "What the fuck, over?" And that's my question today to the etymologists at Oxford.

May 3   𝔉romage, d'Angleterre

I'm eating Huntsman cheese, which is double Gloucester with strips of Stilton in between. How is this stuff not a controlled substance? What is the DEA focused on anyway?

May 4   **Big Sky Country**

I had occasion to meet then-Montana Governor Brian Schweitzer at a Billings press conference for my employer, GE. Montana press conferences are genteel affairs featuring the softest ball questions ever posed by The Fourth Estate.

Having arrived on a Gulfstream V corporate jet, my East Coast superiority was piquant. Schweitzer is a giant of a man, all glad-handing and easy chitchat, in cowboy boots and bolo tie. A one-dimensional hayseed, I concluded.

Chatting before the event, I mentioned that my son was living in Damascus, volunteering for the UN. The Governor casually mentioned he speaks fluent Arabic and has done business with Arabs for years. "Wonderful people," he said. "A fascinating culture. I spent a lot of time in the Kingdom."

My smugness got a timeout.

May 5   **Salt or No Salt?**

Me in my GE Capital office paying visual tribute to a famous Mexican holiday. The photo is emblematic of a cerebral comedic sensibility – the kind Noel Coward or Stephen Fry would envy.

May 6 **Bang!**

Dr Richard Gatling believed his weapon, the forerunner of the machine gun, would actually reduce battlefield deaths. Because of its lethality, he reasoned, soldiers would be unwilling to fight. Dr Guillotine regarded his device as a humanitarian advance too. Both men were physicians.

May 7 **Do as You're Told**

A Facebook group administrator spoke to me sharpish today. "Stick to the script," on her page or be summarily booted out. "You can start your own page." Her page, her rules, however small-minded, dull and repetitive. Fair enough, but she got me thinking.

I've always struggled to escape the tepid script I'd been given. I didn't want to conform and I didn't want to fit in. I saw a different story line. My intellectual curiosity wasn't much, but I enjoyed it, muddled and undisciplined though it was. I overreached all the time, but at least I tried. Stick to the script? Nah, I'd rather be a stone in your shoe.

May 8 **Dirty Talk**

Elsewhere a long thread discussed slang terms for the human sexual apparatus and sexual acts. Emotions ran high and comments reflect strong personal feelings. However there's one thing we, as ladies and gentlemen of intellectual refinement, can agree on. The expression "driving the meat bus to tuna town" is not cool.

May 9   **The Blood of the Russians**

Every year on this day, Mother Russia celebrates the end of WW II. Here's why it matters still. In 1978, the Archbishop of Canterbury went on an official visit to that vast land. In church after church, the prelate told me over drinks, grandmothers in their babushka scarfs turned out in the hundreds.

Finally, in exasperation, he asked why no men ever came to worship. "Oh, there are no men. They're all dead, you see, killed in the war," the priest was told. Churchill said WW II was won with the manufacturing might of the Americans, the intelligence successes of the British (decoding Enigma for instance) – and the blood of the Russians. And that still touches hearts from St Petersburg right the way to Vladivostok.

May 10   **The Motherland**

This photo from The NYTs is so quintessentially, so beautifully, so hauntingly Russian – a funeral for a much-loved war hero in a snowstorm.

May 11   **Shut Up and Sing**

I caused a _contretemps_ by posting a Seinfeld joke about Lady Gaga, a popular performer. The joke was, "I hate Lady Gaga. She's one letter away from being Lady Gag".

Fans leapt to her defense, believing I harbour her ill will. I do not and my mea culpa is reproduced here for your edification.

> _Dear Lords, Ladies and Gentlemen,_
>
> _I have no feelings for or against Ms Gaga. I'm glad she got her dogs back because they're worth as much as Bill Gates's sock drawer and her taste in meat-based eveningwear is unsurpassed._
>
> _I remain Yrs Faithfully,_
>
> _JPV Oliver, Gent_

May 12   **90 Days to Word Power**

A friend asked me to use "foppish" in a sentence. My effort follows.

> Nigel charbroiled the fresh-caught pink foppish to perfection simultaneously sautéing the sartorial, ripe and glistening, in garlic and butter, catching the sleeve of his Madder silk dressing gown alight only twice, whilst Mahler wafted from the wireless so fortissimo that when he, Nigel, declared their late supper at its apogee and opened the Pol Roger, Vivian was teetering from her third Gin cocktail and could

not help but wonder where the tartar sauce had got to.

[NOTE: Students of Cockney rhyming slang will grasp the meaning behind my choice of preparation for the "foppish". Sartorial is a popular fish in Southeast Asia.]

May 13   **ℐNYSCHSA**

Saratoga Springs, NY, is redolent with history and hostelries – the Battles of Saratoga being chief among them and, at one time, the city was home to the largest hotels on Earth. As a child, for example, I learnt of the fabled Highway Superintendent Association, as all children do, but never dreamt I would actually live near its hallowed ground, now the site of The Spa City Motor Lodge. The past here sparkles like so many diamonds.

May 14   **Chirp, Tweet, Flap**

An encounter with a person of a certain political persuasion today reminds me that arguing with American Conservatives is like playing chess with a pigeon. The bird clucks incoherently, shits all over the board and then stomps around like he won the game.

May 15   # HM The Queen

This a 1985 picture of Mrs Cornelius Vanderbilt Whitney (1925 - 2019) and me at her apartment on 59th and 5th in Manhattan. Over my shoulder is The Plaza Hotel, the golden statue of General William Tecumseh Sherman by St Gaudens and Central Park. Known to one and all as Marylou, Mrs. Whitney was an icon in the thorough-

bred racing world, a philanthropist and the long-reigning Queen of Saratoga society. I appear dubious of her drink-making skills, but she was a complete delight and hugely clever. When my son was born, she sent him a Tiffany piggy bank. Now that's funny.

May 16   # A Healthy Body

The WSJ reports over 57 million Americans belong to a health club. We know this because those people never shut up about it. The body-conscious Greeks invented gyms and the word gymnasion means "school for naked exercise", a place to refine patriotic ideals and working on your quads. If you're among the 57 million, and your nasty bits aren't dangling free on the StairMaster, you're doing it wrong. Slip off your Spandex and Greek it – just wipe the machine down when you're done.

May 17   **Medium Rare Gwen**

There are two places to get serious steaks in Saratoga. One is the Spa City Farmers' Market every Sunday morning, held on the grounds of The Lincoln Baths. My favorite vendor is Lisa Saunders from Saunders Family Farm, Greenwich, NY, who brings in meats various. Mrs Saunders's Delmonicos are out of this world and the only downside is she names the animals. Yesterday for dinner, for example, I dined on Cindy or Josey – I forget which really.

The other place is 15 Church, easily the best restaurant in town. Before going, take stock because your life is about to change. You shall see all other eateries as second-rate. It is sublime.

May 18   **The Thunderbirds**

In WW II, my father was a Master Sergeant in the US Army's 45th Infantry Division, formerly an Oklahoma National Guard unit. It was largely composed of Native Americans and, at the war's start, the War Office decreed they had to change their shoulder patch design. It was felt their ancient symbol, the swastika, could be confusing.

May 19   **Unguents, Salves, Balms and Ointments**

In Britain, Oil of Olay, an anti-aging skin cream, used to be called Oil of Ulay. To English ears, olay sounded like what the *Picador* shouts in a bullfight, but the product is now marketed around the world as Olay (no Oil of).

It contains trieathanolamine, hydroxyisohexyl 3-cyclo-hexhene carboxaldehyde, butylphenyl methlypropinate – which sure sounds like an epic weekend to me. For perfect skin, you could also try no sun, no gin, lots of sleep and kale-based clothing. I wouldn't, but you could.

May 20   **Occupied**

The world's best post-poop butt cleaning device is a Japanese toilet seat. You choose the type, intensity, direction and temperature of the water spray. The seat is heated. It is a thoroughly pleasant experience. You choose the music too – I always "go" with Bizet. Get it? One joke, two punch lines. Ha. Ha.

But since you don't know the Japanese word for STOP, you won't be able to shut the fucking thing off. This will flood your 5 Star Tokyo hotel suite, discommoding the nice newlyweds from Osaka in the room beneath you. You will become unpopular in the hotel bar. The unflappable Japanese concierge will come close to flapping. It will be a thoroughly unpleasant experience, but your hiney will be happy. Now finish your *saki*.

May 21   **Canes, Canines and Cubanos**

I got this handsome walking stick at Dunhill Tobacconists in St James's, London.

The head reminded me of my beloved dog, Buckminster, who'd only recently shuffled off his mortal coil. With the cane and a box of *Monte Cristos* #3, the bill was

stratospheric, but one paid no heed to trifles.

The cane has come into actual use now since I am beset by one of the thousand slings and arrows that flesh is heir to. Buck is at my side again, in spirit, keeping me on an even keel. He was a better, more affectionate and more patient dog than I deserved.

May 22   ## But Was He?

This true man of the Scottish Enlightenment died some 220 years ago. He was friends with Adam Smith and The National Bard of Scotland Robert Burns wrote a poem in his honour. Burns's first volume of works was printed in his publishing house. He created The Society of Antiquaries of Scotland and The Royal Society of Scotland.

He compiled and edited the **Encyclopaedia Britannica**. His translation into English of **Histoire Naturalle** became a best seller. In the 19th Century, his two volume set of **The Philosophy of Natural History** was required reading at Harvard. His papers are archived in the library of The National Museum of Scotland. Such was his wit, people sought him for their dinner parties.

His name was William Smellie.

May 23 **Champagne, Strawberries and Cream**

Once, in a summer of the Kentish countryside, I met a high-caste Englishwoman, a vertiginous blonde of dignity and bearing. It was she for whom the expression *de haut en bas* was invented. She told me forthrightly the bags beneath my eyes and my potbelly were my most prominent features. Furthermore she said she quite liked these because they suggested a louche and debauched nature. It's the nicest thing anybody ever said to me. She'd effin love me now.

May 24

"What is there in the moon that should move my heart so potently?"

- John Keats (1795 – 1821)

May 25 **D'Excès is its Own Reward**

Restaurants, which have the highest rate of failure in the small business category, expand and contract like the human heart. As an impoverished graduate student in England, circa 1978, I engaged in two breathtaking extravagances.

The first was at a posh steakhouse in London's Mayfair district. That eatery, The Guinea Grill, 30 Bruton Place, lustily displayed gleaming Scotch beef on butcher blocks. My steak-starved appetite went mad and living on tea and cheese for the next three days was well worth it.

The other was The Duck Inn in Pett Bottom, south of Canterbury. That night our taxi driver lurked his way through a dense fog in deepest, darkest rural Kent. The cuisine was transcendently French, the wine too. Pett Bottom is the village where Ian Fleming's James Bond stayed for a time with his aunt (we saw neither). After that meal, I couldn't afford tea or cheese. Both of these establishments are still up and running 40 plus years on. Tell 'em I sent you.

May 26   **The Ends, the Means**

With the English language, you can have both caruncles and carbuncles.

George Washington, for instance, had caruncles - just as you and I do - and, on the presidential bottom, enormous carbuncles which made horseback riding tortuous. We can thus deduce The Father of Our Nation's unsmiling portraits may have less to do with dentation and more to do with his pasty, white, mottled, sagging, sweaty, fetid, veined and pustulent hiney.

HRH Prince Charles, about whose bottom we know precious little, is a thoughtful student of architecture. He once described a futuristic tower going up in Central London as a "carbuncle on the face of an old friend". The design doubtless inflamed his caruncles.

May 27   **Sit, Write Here.**

Gail M. Stein
Frozen Moments

May 28   **Domestic Discord**

It's a busy day here at Chateau Oliver. The entire house-hold is to decamp to MacGowan Abbey, my family's ances-tral estate nestled deep in the wilds of Canada, for the remainder of the summer. Finial is newly returned to his post and our current undertaking requires all the orga-nization skills and discipline he possesses. It's quite the caravan, what with cases of silver polish, Laphroaig, three barnsful of livestock, etc.

Whilst it's good to have my butler managing things, there's a brooding subplot at work. His termagant wife, Margaret Mary Siobhan, against whom I have a judicial order of protection, is sowing discord among the village's more impressionable gentlefolk, telling these gorpish innocents I'm a Conservative Republican, a despicable falsehood on the face of it. I shall seek redress in The Courts.

Of a morning before The Plague, she got into the cooking sherry, became emotionally upset and – I'm abashed to tell you this – threatened me with the business end of a skillet. *In my own library!* She may be a dab hand at puddings, but alcohol is not her friend.

May 29   **You Live Where?**

The English County of Kent, where I lived for a time, has funny place names.

For example, The Hundred of Hoo is not to be confused with The Hundred of Shamel. The Weald of Kent boasts a lovely golf course. You can, in that County, also find the Lath of Aylesford, but you need to move east from Sheerness.

England also had Grumbald's Ash, in Gloucestershire, till the late 19th Century, which was home to Chipping Sodbury and Didmarton. Nobody remembers what Marton did, but they kept the name anyway. All these were in the Lower Division, as any schoolchild can tell you. The world marvels at the eccentricities of English. They drink too much tea, that's what I think.

May 30

"Throw away thy rod
Throw away thy wrath
O my God
Take the gentle path"

- English poet George Herbert circa 1625.

May 31 **Onward Christian Soldiers**

One Memorial Day, the 400-strong Corps of Cadets of *l'Ecole Militaire* mustered on a side street for a big parade down Albany's Central Avenue. At the bugle's sound to step off, 30 or so Cadets tumbled out of a nearby gin mill, their brass shined, shoes polished, caps on straight, rifles in hand and beer on their breath.

Pictured is Company H, commanded by my best friend of 50 years, Captain Michael Lodington Soares, USN (Ret). He died in December 2019.

June 1 **Kiss My Air**

There's a sameness to society events. *Tout* Saratoga turned out for the season opener a year ago tonight on the patio of 15 Church, the town's finest eatery and the evening did not disappoint. Overdressed women in tight print dresses and men in Brooks Brothers jackets and $190 jeans. The desire to see and be seen, fresh from the tanning booth, was intense; you could feel it.

The night's *soirée* included a rare and precious gift: two wealthy dames in the identical outfit. This was first noticed by my *fiancée*-to-be, The Hon Leesa Perazzo.

The two gals, who pawed about languidly occasionally snarling for dominance on the 15 Church *Serengeti*, seemed oblivious to the *faux pas*. Artful photographer and author, Richard Lovrich, knew he'd struck society gold and delighted in getting just the right shot – as he always does. Another Chardonnay?

June 2   Interview Magazine

On that long ago June morning at The Tavern on the Green, Andy Warhol gently held out a copy his magazine to me. Wordless, tiny, fragile, he looked like somebody who nearly died from a gunshot wound, which he was. His companion, a bosomy redhead, prolix, sturdy, loud, wanted you to know. He hadn't been invited to my PR event, but everybody quite liked that he was there. By that time in his career, he was a "business artist".

We then climbed into our 19th Century carriages – four horsepower, candles in the lamps, footmen to the rear – dozens of them, and headed for The Seagram Building, leaving Andy and The Tall Redhead behind. He would die two years later following botched gall bladder surgery.

The entire day was surreal. 1985 Midtown Manhattan demanded to know why its innocent byways had been snarled with an invasion of four-in-hands from 1828 England. "A publicity stunt," I offered meekly. Such are the joys of the propagandist.

June 3   Bottoms Up!

Reader Janet from Seven Oaks in the UK, writes, "JPV, you're so gosh darned sophisticated, what's the correct way to drink Sherry?"

Great question, Janet! Any kind of small crystal glass is acceptable, but there's a strict formality to proper Sherry drinking.

First, pour the gleaming nectar very slowly into the

glass. Be sure the room's ambient light is strong so you can see the colour clearly. Gently swirl the Sherry around. This will release its particular aromas. Nose the beverage thoughtfully and write down what occurs to you. This next bit must be followed precisely. Take the glass in your right hand walk carefully to the sink. Flip the glass upside down in one fluid motion. Then get in your motor, drive directly to Odd Bins, buy Laphroaig, have three sips to clear your mind and return home. You and the whisky glass will be much happier.

June 4   𝓗at 𝓗ead 𝓣ypist

I have two small collections - hats and typewriters.

My tar bucket from military school is here, as is a Coke hat – a proto-hardhat for 18th Century construction sites. A pith helmet honors Dr David Livingstone, whom you should look up. An East German Army helmet recalls the gory Cold War photo of a private who, trying to defect by leaping over the Berlin Wall, was shot dead.

A Swiss postman's hat marks a man of authority, as does the headwear of a Pashtun elder. A cheap baseball cap celebrates the US$63 million legal verdict for GE and Bechtel concerning the Dahbol Powerplant in Maharashtra, India. Thousands of impoverished fishermen and their families were "relocated". The hat is triumphant. There are others.

The typewriters tell stories too. As a boy of 11, I used my father's 1930s machine to write to Lock and Co Hatters, St James's, London, about buying a Bowler hat. They were gracious in reply. The prize of this group is The Oliver, a bizarrely designed device around 1912.

Its creator, a Methodist minister, Mr Oliver (no relation), was excoriated for leaving his flock to pursue mammon. It was thought the Devil's own work when, in 1918, Rev Oliver sold his company for the breathtaking sum of $100,000. There are others.

June 5   A Tin of Austerity

Turnbull and Asser is an upmarket shop for dress shirts and ties on London's famed row of shirt makers, Jermyn Street. A T & A clerk, with the most perfect beard you've ever seen, once upbraided me for mentioning that HRH Prince Philip's collar was frayed when I met him.

"In this country, Sir, when something is old, we get it repaired!" which he spat through clenched teeth. Americans don't grasp the grinding poverty Brits endured after WW II – and those memories linger. Shirt collars were the least of it. A senior GE guy's father was a London tailor. "It was simple," he said. "If he didn't work, we didn't eat."

June 6   Lordy, Lordy

"Awaiting Her Majesty was the ghastly, fake, Brexit-hating, pocket-filling, claret-gargling, *cliché*-spouting modern House of Lords: a worm-farm of *bien pensant* quangocrats,

activist judges, busybodies, fallen stooges, ex-MPs and a few last mouldering viscounts."
— Quentin Letts in The Daily Mail on the 2019 State Opening of Parliament

June 7 **Garson and Ruth**

For millions of people, the cult classic **Harold and Maude** is unforgettable cinema. A few years after its release, I went to a talk Ruth Gordon gave here in Saratoga Springs. She was as magical and wonderful as you'd expect and the audience was smitten, but in the middle of the presentation, I needed a bio break.

Standing alone in the lobby, smoking a cigarette, was her husband, playwright Garson Kanin. I praised his wife's performance. "Yeah," he growled, "the woman never shuts up."

June 8 **Four Olivers Drumming**

My father, me and my son played the drums in the cellar of the Pink Palace. What we lacked in talent, which was much, we made up for in volume. On the night of the 1964 Great American Blackout, I was playing. As the lights flickered, my mother threw open the cellar door and demanded I desist. She believed I was causing the power grid of

the Northeastern United States to fail.

In fifth grade, my beloved daughter, Emily, carried on the family tradition. One night she was flailing away in an ear-splitting blur of sticks. "What are you playing, Emma?" I asked gently. "Oh that's Mozart's Sonata in D Major," she replied with evident pride. My younger daughter, Mary, being the wisest of the bunch, has opted for the ukulele – and she's quite good.

June 9   **Lunch?**

One work day while I was at Seagram, we decided to head to Laurent Restaurant, a few blocks to the north, on East 56th Street, just in from Park Avenue.

At the next table, sat six ominous chaps including Mob boss, John "The Dapper Don" Gotti, then head of the Gambino crime family.

The Don sat with his back to the room, but he watched everybody who came in via the giant mirror on the wall.

Each of his colleagues looked like the movie thugs you'd expect. Each seemed to have been sent by Central Casting.

The public never saw Laurent's stunning and ancient wine cellar, which occupied three levels beneath the sparkling dining room.

The first bin of wines was labeled "Richard Burton", the next "Elizabeth Taylor". As you descended the rickety steps, celebrity names became more and more antiquated.

Clark Gables' 25 priceless clarets waited futilely in the dust for their long-dead owner.

June 10   A Secondary Education

Many people are rightly fond of their high school memories. In contrast, my class at *l'Ecole Militaire* voted me Most Likely to Someday Explain His Actions to a Court-Appointed Psychiatrist. In fairness it was a tough school. When the teacher asked what followed a sentence, the cadet would say an appeal. Cadets stole hubcaps from moving cars. Tough school, I tell ya. The school newspaper had an obituary column. Thanks, Rodney.

June 11   And Yĕ Shall Receive

I was today asked to address five questions about me. Herewith, the replies.

- I was born in 1922 in the Principality of Andorra on a snowy August night. My mother never wanted to breastfeed; she said she only liked me as a friend.
- I was for a time a veterinarian proctologist, specializing in horses asses.
- My favourite milkshake is Cream of Mushroom.
- I have a pet piranha named Munches. He *really* does not like to be touched.
- My favourite colour is plaid.

June 12   I Once Had a Voice Coach in Africa

In the 1985 film, **Out of Africa**, Robert Redford played a dashing English aristocrat, adventurer and big game hunter. When director Sidney Pollack heard Redford's risible English accent, he decided this quintessentially British character would, in fact, be an American – with the ordinary Yank name of Denys Finch Hatton.

June 13   **England and the English**

Many North Americans go to England for their summer vacation ("wanktrip" in British English). Here are some English words actual English people say. Using these words will identify you as worldly and "in-the-know".

BREXIT: This is how the English pronounce the word breakfast. As in, "I say, Gwen, might you enjoy a full Brexit this lovely summer morning?"
"Quite, Roderick, I want you to give me a big, hot, steaming Brexit – with bangers," Gwen murmured coquettishly. Bangers are sausages; don't be smutty.

PIKEY: A term of enormous affection and respect. "Now that I see your lovely home, Alastair, I realise just how pikey you really are." [Note the incorrect spelling of realize. If you mention their chronic spelling errors, the English become emotionally upset.]

PUNNET: Since they live in a Socialist country, the English never have to work and they just stay home all day making-up silly words. As in, "Clive, where did you put the punnet of strawberries? And for god sakes, stop drinking Pimm's out of the flagon". Punnet is synonymous with luggage.

QUANGO: This is a deliciously tart fruit from some little tropical country England used to own. Asking for a quango and gin suggests sophistication.

PRO TIP: The English are just North Americans with adorable accents. You can usually be understood by these quaint natives, but always speak more loudly than you do at home. Also, be sure to dress like you're in the cast of Downton Abbey. All English people dress this way and are forever "being handed a note" while rogering the scullery maid. Rogering the scullery maid is the national pastime of England.

ROGER: A verb meaning to gently scold an inferior for a slight misdeed. As in, "Please stay but a little, Quentin. I must administer a quick rogering, old fruit."

As they say in Gloucestershire, *Bon Voyage*!

June 14   **Especially in a Plague**

At Chateau Oliver, we have the habit of gracious living and norms of decorum are strictly observed. Just now my trusted valet, Finial, decanted a 40-year-old bottle of claret with the bottle's neck over a small candle. In this way, no sediment gets into the wine glass. One hopes the bucket of crispy KFC is up to the challenge.

June 15   **Errata**

Describing how to decant a bottle of claret, either I or spellcheck wrote sentiment when sediment was the proper word. Readers swooped in and the correction was made. Writers are conversant with typos, those muscular, noxious weeds in the garden of prose. I pledge to you now, hand-on-heart, that such mistakes shall never, ever again appear in my writing. I solemnly promise that, in these pages, typos are a thing of the pass.

June 16   One Day in Provence

In the charming village of *Chateauneuf de Pape* in the Rhône Vallée, 2010. The shopkeeper eccentrically argued the wine was better warmed up.

June 17   Three, Two, One...

When I was 11, I got a library book that explained how to hypnotize somebody.

My brother was my first – and as it turned out, only – subject. In short order, he was on the living room couch hypnotized. Our mother was unlettered and deeply super-stitious. For example, she believed cats are actual Earthly instruments of the Devil – a reasonable view when you consider what dipshits cats are.

As I issued modest commands to my sibling, she strolled in and freaked out. Mother concluded I'd reduced her youngest child to an irreversible vegetative state, so I woke him up, calmed her down, returned the library book and promised to never again use my powers for evil. It was an ordinary Thursday in June around The Pink Palace.

June 18   Columbia County Spirits

With my second family – Michael Lodington Soares, whom I met in *l'Ecole Militaire*, and his mother, whom I called Mumsie. We're shown at their home in North Chatham, NY, the day she graduated from college. She was 75.

June 19   JKG and India

In 2020, twenty Indian soldiers died in a clash with Chinese forces in the Ladakh region. No shots were fired – it was brutal and blood-soaked hand-to-hand combat. The two nations actually went to war over the land in 1962, when JFK's ambassador to India was John Kenneth Galbraith.

Kennedy always read JKG's cables, not because he was especially interested in the subcontinent. The President read them because Galbraith was such a captivating writer. In fact, Galbraith's messages got attention at both State and the WH just on the strength of his prose and if you've not read his memoirs, you're in for a treat.

June 20   Teary-Eyed

When my children were little, I'd read them bits of books I love. This was especially effective by candlelight when the power went out in darkest rural Connecticut. **The Pickwick Papers** was chief among these works and Jingle's introduction, for instance, always got laughs. One recent Father's Day, two thirds of my progeny visited, my poetical daughters Emily and Mary. They asked for Dickens who, of course, gets academic guff for sentimentality.

My reading that night – from later in the novel – was halted from time to time by emotion (mine). This happens more as I age. Perhaps it's weakness or perhaps I'm sentimental. Forgive me; we live in a confessional epoch. If you come over some day, I'll read to you too if you'd like. Expect pauses.

June 21   # Sallow and Callow

In undergraduate school, I managed the college radio station, "WOWI Radio – Where College Rock Originates." We'd have had more listeners by shouting out of the window.

June 22   # Enough with the Smiting Already

The divide between the Old Testament and New is clear. Once God had a kid, He mellowed right out and was all, like, peace and love, Dude. Some people say it was the pot, but I think having a family gave Him perspective.

Oh, and The Holy Ghost got on Zoloft, which made a big difference. Also the success of His religions, which are the only true religions, helped with His mood, what with all that worship, adoration, praise and sacred music rolling in every weekend.

Fact: Christianity has three top gods, but really only one and Christians contort themselves into celestial pretzels explaining how they're not polytheists.

June 23   **Historiography**

Alan Cowell wrote a piece in The NYTs on Jews in modern day Germany. His first sentence is a mastery of concision.

"BERLIN: The past lurks here like a tripwire."

June 24   **A Public Service**

I had oral surgery a year ago today. As an expert *du vin et alcool*, I knew what paired best with Vicodin and antibiotics. A 1964 *Pol Roger* for the starter course, well-chilled *Batard Montrechet* with the main – lightly-breaded flounder if memory serves – and three snifters of Martell VSOP post-prandially. Some might argue for Hennessy XO as the digestif, but that would ignore the imbalance in that cognac's *bon bois et fin bois*. To say nothing of its aggressive *bois ordinaire*.

June 25   "My Point is..."

I always hold forth in Scottish pubs, just not always coherently. Everyone, you see, is entitled to my opinion. The Sheep Heid Inn, Duddingston, Edinburgh.

June 26   Rosin Your Bow

There's much to recommend in Saratoga Springs – nine museums, numberless pubs and restaurants, hotels to luxuriate in, shops great and small, two superb colleges, art galleries, laughter, the storied flat track, the harness track and a clattering casino.

Buskers were not on the list, until today. A young woman in a summer dress played the violin on Broadway in the warm sunlight. Her gentle music made the roaring trucks sick and pale with grief.

June 27   Happy Chem Trails to You

Stuffed Trigger, wax Roy Rogers with stuffed Bullet in the background. May you be forever as delighted as Wax Roy.

Just avoid open flame and prolonged direct sunlight. Photo credit: Wax Dale Evans.

June 28   **Breathe Deep**

Saratoga Springs boasts endless ways to diminish your bank account, two bookshops you won't want to leave, the best crepes outside Marseille, an ATM that'll give you $s for 99 cents, a lobster roll they write sonnets about and the most expensive horse shit on the planet.

Thoroughbreds are here pooping vigorously, but, because of The Plague, there are no spectators, no queues and lots of vacant hotel rooms. Bring wellies, a pitchfork, a wheelbarrow, credit cards and all the cash you have. Your garden will love you.

June 29   **Smoother Operator**

Whilst running on a treadmill in a public gymnasium a life-time or two ago, a highly decorative young woman chose to occupy the rowing machine adjacent. I glanced her way one nanosecond too long.

My right foot landed on the rim of the device and I flew backward with blinding speed, limbs and Nikes flailing in a jumble, coming to rest in a sweaty heap, moaning. "You OK, Sir?" the comely rower asked. "Sir?" There was not an atom of dignity remaining.

June 30   **Scowlership**

There are thousands of people who can better explain the notion in Literary Criticism called The Selective Fallacy. But, even with my dust-laden third-rate undergraduate degree, I'll give it a whirl.

The guilty academic, student (or Trump supporter) chooses only arguments and data points that support his or her abundantly goofy thesis. He or she does this because his or her thesis is oafish to begin with. Such a grave error – for obvious reasons – calls into question not only the scholarship, but the mental stability, of such a person.

Anyone dim enough to commit The Selective Fallacy achieves a high ranking on The International Stupid Scale, published quarterly by *The Pohjoisesplanadi Group*, a Helsinki-based think-tank I just made up.

The Selective Fallacy resides in the English department. Selective Bias is for those hippies in the Sociology building.

July 1   **Happy Canada Day**

In 1815, my Scottish ancestors sailed to North America because they heard you could drink Canada dry. They also left Scotland because the King's soldiers had really pointy bayonets. According to HM, the Olivers were, and I'm quoting here, *Failed Scottish Peasants*. In the 19th Century's social pecking order, this was no mean feat. Still they thrived here. Well, anyhoo, that's the story. What was I meant to talk about? Something about legal pot?

July 2   **There'll Always Be an...**

Britain's been going through a lot – the Plague, Brexit, the Royals' daily slugfest, Bojo's annoying coiffure, Scottish independence, the continued existence of Jacob Rees-Mogg and How Important is the Brecon and Radnorshire By-Election really? I here suggest a way to calm Britannic waters: just rename the nation something zippy and new. Something modern sensibilities will fancy. A big step, but hear me out.

The name, Ladies and Gentlemen, is *The Peoples' Republic of Tukogbani*, home to a young, vibrant and sexy regime run by "wild-eyed pistol-wavers who ain't afraid to die". The name is an acronym of The United Kingdom of Great Britain and Northern Ireland. Let's face it, the United Kingdom has been neither united nor a kingdom for decades. Plus, the UK sounds like they just totally copied the US.

July 3 — The Spirit of '76!

Tomorrow Americans like me celebrate our hard-won independence over 200 years ago. People in every nation however can look back in awe at Adam Smith's **Wealth of Nations**, published that same year. A work of breathtaking accomplishment, it presaged the modern economic world, opened 18th Century eyes to the division of labor and free markets and much else besides. Mr Smith was a Scottish academic who lived with his mother. God bless America. Scotland forever.

July 4 — The Fourth of July

Each man who signed the Declaration of Independence knew if things didn't go well, he'd dangle at the end of a rope. Some signatures are more memorable than others.

"We have it in our power to begin the world over again."

- Thomas Paine, Common Sense, 1776

That is the essence, the beating heart, of the American Experiment. The Declaration was a team effort. For example, in a draft, Jefferson wrote, "We hold these truths to be sacred". Franklin, an Enlightenment man of science, crossed out sacred and wrote "self-evident" in its place.

The word for this American foundation is consanguinity. It appears in the Declaration.

"They too have been deaf to the voice of justice and of consanguinity." The Americans were telling the English, "We're family. Don't you get it? We're the same blood. We're kin". Some in Parliament supported the Americans, but HM's government did not get it. So the Colonies took on the greatest power on Earth.

"We pledge our lives, our Fortunes and our sacred honour to this Declaration," they wrote.

"American Exceptionalism", by contrast, is an insipid notion used by the Right to justify all manner of arrogance, rapaciousness and thuggery. The distinction between the two phrases is hugely important. We've had in our history darker times than 2017 to 2020, but none so intellectually bankrupt and insulting to our ideals as a nation.

July 5   **Play Ball!**

The Hon Leesa Perazzo and me at The Otesaga Hotel at the 4th of July, 2020, weekend. In the long, storied history of Cooperstown, NY, no two people ever possessed less interest in baseball than we.

July 6

This Goodly Frame the Earth

An exquisite ride on Amtrak of a faultless summer morning, from Albany to Manhattan. Nature cares not for The Plague; it cares for sun-drenched watercolors and the Hudson's shimmering, painterly beauty.

July 7

A Wee Dram?

In 1983, my shambolic life was made into a movie called **Ruben, Ruben**. The producers didn't intend to do this and I signed no consent forms. It featured the sublime Tom Conti as Gowan McGland, a bibulous and louche Scots poet, all tweeds and whisky, who falls hard for a much younger woman. The story is from a novel by my favorite writer, Peter de Vries. Way too close to home for yours truly; even now, viewing it brings fat tears.

July 8

The Thrill of Victory

I spent the last couple of days in Lake Placid, NY, one of America's two Olympic training centers. The facilities were glamorous, the weather sublime. I was especially proud to – at long last – join the storied United States

Olympic Jumping Team and I showed up fully kitted-out. My IRH Medalist Velveteen Hunter Jumper riding helmet and Ariat tall boots gleamed. My spurs were of the first rank, my show coat tailored to perfection. The *Devoucoux* saddle was handcrafted in *Biarritz*, as you'd expect.

Triumph soon turned to heartbreak, however, when I was told my four-legged friend did not qualify for competition.

My beloved yak, Jenny, and I were forced to lumber off into the sunset, mocking laughter ringing our ears, decades of work for naught. The dream was shattered, her hairy tail tucked between her formidable hind legs. Jenny's polished cloven hooves caught the late day sunlight as we left The Olympic Training Center. We now know only the agony of defeat. I steadied myself for the lonely trip home with a steaming pint of fresh yak milk, warm from Jenny's teat.

July 9   Tally Ho No!

The Garden of England was a feast for the eyes, especially at the height of summer. Motoring about the Kentish countryside one July day, when fox hunts were still legal, a friend and I had to stop the car as a big hunt crossed the rural lane.

It was picture perfect – red jackets, tall boots, gleaming brass, yelping hounds, a bugler, the lot, the scene framed by fields of deep green. It took a while for the riders to make their way. At long last, we started to inch forward but had to stop instantly. The hunt was followed by an equally large group of sign-wielding protesters.

The unspeakable in pursuit of the uneatable were themselves pursued.

July 10   **Real Ale**

When I was a young man, I drove a Hedrick's Beer truck in Albany, NY. It was my father's tiny distributorship and the lager was dreadful. The O'Connell Political Machine owned the brewery – and New York State's capital city for 60 years or so. These were not craft brewers. Once, when a sample got sent to the lab, the report said, "To Whom It May Concern, Your horse has diabetes." That's a bad beer. Of a Saturday, a regular customer came to my father's shop for his weekly keg of Hedrick's. The man's late-stage cirrhosis was of little notice.

July 11   **Winey**

In my time at Seagram, I often encountered Frank Prial, then the wine columnist at The NYTs. His column ran in the paper for 25 years and he was a classic newspaper-man. Prial argued many great wines aren't really great, but trade on posh labels and past glories.

He told me how to deal with a wine snob, often a silver-throated macaw from North Jersey who corners you at a dinner party and holds forth with his enological genius.

"Just tell him the wine of the evening died on the middle palate," Prial advised. "The guy will shut right up." In the wine business, the collective noun for such people is "hobbyists", not a term of affection.

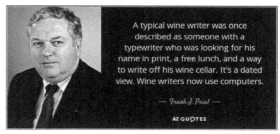

A typical wine writer was once described as someone with a typewriter who was looking for his name in print, a free lunch, and a way to write off his wine cellar. It's a dated view. Wine writers now use computers.

— *Frank J. Prial* —

AZ QUOTES

July 12   𝔉ish 𝔉ood

Because it's extravagantly expensive, eating Russian caviar is memorable. For me the most noteworthy of such events occurred in 1988 38,000 feet above the Pacific. Seagram, my employer, allowed me to take a few hundred parents of American Olympians to Seoul for the Summer Games.

To accomplish this, I leased a 747, never mind that my signing authority permitted no such thing. On the journey home, an athlete's mother came into First Class to say thanks for our largess and she was directed to my seat. The woman had a gift for me – a tin of Beluga caviar straight from the Caspian.

"My daughter's on the US Equestrian team and she's thrilled her father and I got to see her compete," she said as we consumed her fish eggs, washed down with good Russian vodka. I complimented her wildly expensive Nikon. Rich people, I thought.

"Oh, that my neighbor's camera – we're completely broke. Every penny we ever had went into my daughter's training." I poured her another vodka and, in the fullness of time, wished her a good night's sleep 38,000 feet above the Pacific.

July 13   𝔗he 𝔅artender

Joseph Kennah of Judson Street, Albany, NY, decided he would not be fighting in The Great War for the Americans or anybody else, so on a hunting trip to the Helderberg Escarpment in the rainy and cold autumn of 1917, a rifle blast removed his great toe from his left foot. He was 17.

Uncle Joe never told my brother and me, but we knew. He took us on hikes into the Adirondack forest and long before the "scenic highway", we climbed Prospect Mountain near the Village of Lake George. He told us ghost stories and let me fire his over-under shotgun. My brother and I occupied a special section of the big house called Seventh Heaven, just down the hall from the Black cooks who worked in Uncle Joe's restaurant. He claimed to have been shot in the chest during a bar brawl, but his silk shirt saved him, silk being bullet proof.

Years earlier, he owned a Hedrick's Beer distributorship in Albany, but got caught cheating The O'Connell Political Machine. The O'Connells owned the brewery, the police, the rackets and much else besides, so he accepted his new life 60 miles north at Lake George, with a resort property on 70 acres.

After Shirley Temples in his restaurant, Uncle Joe, my parents, my brother and I would head to a little tree behind one of the tourist cabins. Hundred dollar bills were taped to the top, 50s next, then 20s, fives were in reach and coins in piles round the trunk. We could have as much as we could grab. It was The Money Tree, of which he was glee-fully proud and it was, of course, magical to have an uncle like him.

July 14   There They Go!

The last normal opening day at The Race Track was for the 2019 meet. This meant $ 25.95 gin and tonics, men with gold chains round their necks who said, "I'm goin ova ta ha house", women in hats the size of Norway and a slight increase in traffic which locals regarded as catastrophic. We hate when the touristas arrive and we hate when they leave. During The Plague, we hated the silence.

July 15 **Bee Cool**

On this elegant summer evening I sit adjacent to a platoon of honey bees having their hungry way with the Cleome. They're busy, purposeful, charming and they are hard at it.

July 16 **Scold Call**

Yesterday, whilst motoring in sunny New Haven, near Yale, my ill-timed lane change discommoded the corpulent driver of a giant white Cadillac Escalade. Her auto was so huge, it can be seen from outer space. She, on her mobile phone, admonished me with uncivil gesticulations. My whimsical "I Can't Hear You" expression caused the now-enraged motorist to actually fling said cell phone at my car *vigore*. A lesser wit would say her call broke up, but I won't.

July 17 **The Blood of the Lambs**

In 1918, when the Bolsheviks killed Tsar Nicholas II and his family at *Ipatiev* House in *Yekaterinburg*, it took extra effort to kill the children. Pounds and pounds of jewels, sewn into their clothes, acted like bulletproof vests. Not knowing about the jewels, the killers panicked, thinking the girls were protected by magic, maybe even by God himself. A flurry of bayonets and pistols finished the grim work and the Tsar, the Tsarina and their blameless children were dead.

July 18   **On the Boardwalk**

My brother (L) and me in Atlantic City, 1968, when the place was actually posh. My parents took us there every August, starting when I was five. In our suite at the impossibly swank Marlborough-Blenheim Hotel, an antebellum confection, we luxuriated with room service burgers and ice cream. One dressed to stroll on the Boardwalk after 6 pm. Women had to buy special rubber stoppers for their spiked heels so they didn't get caught in the spaces between the boards.

The Diving Bell, The Diving Horse and The Steel Pier were must-sees. My father always got us a stretch limo to motor to Captain Starns' Restaurant. My brother and I occupied the jump seats and struggled with jaw-defeating salt water taffy on the return. We'd then climb into a giant wicker push chair, propelled by an ancient Black man who was full of stories. We'd marvel at the shops on the Boardwalk at night, still picking saltwater taffy from our teeth.

July 19   **Satisfaction**

Eleven years ago today, I met Keith Richards, lead guitarist, Rolling Stones (semi-ret), in the International First Class Lounge, American Airlines, JFK, Queens, NY. He was standing next to me getting a cup of tea at 5.30 on a blisteringly hot Sunday morning. We chatted for seven seconds. You probably expect me to say he looks even more terrifying in person. He does.

Me: Would you like some cream?
KR: Yeah, thanks.

A weak conversationalist, too much bling, reeked of cigarettes, no concept of business casual. Nary a Stratocaster, amplifier or glassine bag of black tar heroin in sight. Don't do drugs, kids.

July 20   **En Pointe**

Some years ago today, a friend and I attended a matinee of the New York City Ballet at the Saratoga Performing Arts Center.

Tiny little girls wore pink tutus, sipped soda and held their mothers' hands while the stage featured an impossible display of athleticism and grace.

For many in the crowd, it rivaled Christmas Day.

Teenagers, sleek and willowy, their hair in ponytails, in groups of three or for, were rapt as dancers defied Issac Newton.

For me, the balletic spectacle, the *grand jeté*, was in the audience. When my friend tried to explain *saut de chats*, I opted for another $18.50 can of Heineken.

July 21

Tennis Anyone?

Some friends and me at The Indian Wells Tennis Resort, California, circa 1987, for a Seagram event (the woman on the far right was real handsy). There was a perfectly legitimate business purpose for all this, as I stipulated in my 12 page annotated expense report. The CFO's audit and comments were excessive.

July 22

Get Me to the Church on Time

One needn't leave an ancient European cathedral to find medieval humour. Sexual and comic carvings are found under statues, benches and in out-of-the-way corners. Stone carvers frequently enjoyed an eternal laugh at the archbishop's expense, a fate I feel sure he richly deserved. Here's a 15th Century statue found in a German cathedral. The masturbating woman's toes are almost curled. From an unpublished photograph in my collection of works by the renowned scholar, medievalist and artist Lester Burbank Bridaham.

July 23   **Splish Splash**

There are spectacularly beautiful bodies of water in and near the vast Adirondack Park of northern New York State. They often have evocative names like Lake Lonely, Lake Tear of The Clouds, Loon Lake, Loughberry Lake and Lake Desolation. My favorite is an off-the-beaten-path one called Lake I Hate Your Guts, Tina. Trout fishing year round. Don't bring Tina.

July 24   **Hamilton, Burr and Burgers**

The former Secretary of the Treasury, Alexander Hamilton, died in 1804, perhaps after deciding not to shoot Aaron Burr, the sitting Vice President of the United States, in a duel who was of course standing at the time. Their feud was profoundly bitter, a frequent feature of gunplay, and

Hamilton called Burr "a voluptuary in the extreme". Burr was never tried for Hamilton's murder, but once you've killed a Founding Father, what's your next career move?

Well, the former vice president immediately thought to run for governor of New York, which tells you a lot about Albany politics (he lost). He then fled to the Southwest territories allegedly in a bid to become emperor of his own country. Burr failed there too and returned to Manhattan, married socialite Eliza Jumel (a former prostitute and one of America's richest women) and practiced law till his death in 1836. A long gone Saratoga pub called Madame Jumel's offered "Brothel Burgers".

July 25   **Obit Dicta**

In a long propaganda career, one writes a lot of different things. In 1988, for example, in the run-up to the Seoul Olympics, fear of Japanese terrorists was so great, I wrote obituaries for the Seagram executives heading to Korea, including me. I had a pretty good life, if my obit's to be believed.

July 26   **Write Aid**

I collect typewriters and this unusual model is one. Mr Oliver was Scots-Canadian, as is my family. He moved to the US and became a Methodist minister in the 1870s because, he moaned, "There's no effin' hockey on TV, eh?" In fact, Rev O created The Oliver Typewriter when he couldn't read his own handwriting. His sermons were a garbled mess, nearly impossible to read which was a blessing for his congregants. The unique design of the machine tells you something very important about the Olivers. Before any design task, we always take LSD.

July 27   

In 1540, Henry VIII executed Thomas Cromwell, who'd been brutal in the dissolution of the monasteries. That was a busy day for the King – in addition to beheading his Lord Great Chamberlain and Lord Privy Seal, he got married. When the wedding photographer took too long, Henry had him decapitated too, which was easy because by that point the executioner was all warmed up.

For three weekends in the winter of 1975, I portrayed Cromwell in a landmark production of *A Man For All Seasons* in Rensselaer, Indiana. My *boffo* star-turn is the stuff of legend in the theater community of northwest Jasper County. Well, not in the entire theater community of northwest Jasper County, of course, but still... The director cast me – and this is true – because, he said, I had an evil face.

July 28   **Reading Entrails**

In a long corporate life like mine, one encounters a steaming cargo load of codswallop. One of the most memorable was the Myers-Briggs Type Indicator. That, er, Indicator is pee-your-pants-laughing lunacy and some of my masters bought it completely. To this day, some people include their four letter code after their name, like an academic designation.

The Magic 8 Ball has greater scientific foundation.

July 29 — Wild Oats

When I was a young man, I briefly dated an extravagantly beautiful woman, a model really, whose husband ran a quote unquote catering business in Newton, Mass. As John Lennon noted in a song lyric, "You could say she was attractively built". Turned out she was the wife of a mob boss – and one day, her chauffeur took me aside.

In a thick Boston accent, he said, "You know, this is, ah, you know, like, gonna end *real* bad for you. I mean, it's up to you, but *you know*...". I wonder how close I came.

July 30 — An Albany Story

This is my father, John J Oliver, on the day of his mother's funeral. She died in the 1918-1919 Influenza Pandemic when he was 10. Nellie Jacobs Oliver was in her early 30s and left her husband, a mentally unstable hypochondriac, with five children, one of whom was two at the time.

My father told of coffins lined up on Albany's Central Avenue sidewalks as far as the eye could see, awaiting their occupants. There was no social safety net, no help from the government, no food programs – only the kindness of friends and family. Those who regard The 2020-2021 Plague and what's followed as a hoax are not students of history – or of anything else for that matter.

July 31   **History Made Easy**

In 1917, The Corfu Declaration created the unified nation of Yugoslavia, but by 1992, everybody agreed "unified" was a poor word choice indeed and they broke the country up into *Yug* and *Slavia*. Historians don't know what happened to the O. The partitioning also created the Republika Srpska, which of course nobody could pronounce so, in 1995, they got rid of that too. After a variety of upheavals, the entire region is now called Lovrichia, which everybody loves, except the Serbs who are always angry about something.

August 1   **City of Light**

Circa 1982, my consort and I dined at *l'Hôtel de Crillon*, in the heart of the *Ancien Régime* in Paris. Wide-eyed and low on *centimes*, I ordered the cheapest bottle from the vast *carte des vins*. An elderly sommelier, expressionless, *tastevin* swaying at mid-torso on his long gray apron, decanted that wine – the bottle's neck over a candle – like it was a '47 *Margaux*.

He never made us feel callow, which was kindness itself. At the next table, a boffin from the US embassy helped American wide-eyed businessmen with their dinner choices. In the shimmering candlelight of the *Ancien Régime*.

August 2   **Unwell**

I knew a family in Westchester County, NY, who described throwing-up as "going number 3". I learned this in the car on a blazing hot August Saturday, taking one of their kids and mine home from a birthday party.

The little boy starts shouting, "*I gotta go NUMBER 3! I gotta go NUMBER 3!*" I didn't know any better, so I told the little fella his joke was really funny. So that's how I learned the expression. I was also reminded of the expression projectile vomiting. It was a long ride home.

August 3   **Kindred Spirits**

In August of 1875, in Ontario, Joseph Hayden Oliver, a Scots Canadian and professional musician, married Margaret Russell MacGowan, who grew up near the Firth of Moray. They'd move to America a year later. In the 1889 US Census, Mrs MacGowan Oliver could fall into one of two categories – a spinster or a widow. She was the latter. Joseph Hayden Oliver was dead.

Here's a photo of my great grandmother with her five children in which she looks brave and lost at the same time. The girl on the right is my Aunt Dora. At 101 and in a nursing home, Dora told me, "Even old people have feelings". I never forgot that. The boy far right is John MacGowan Oliver, my grandfather. Margaret Russell MacGowan Oliver would live to 93, as did my father.

At 90, she'd outlived three of her children and was caring for an 83-year-old woman. Why? "Och aye, cause she needs the help," she'd reply in a lilt all Scotch Mist. Indomitable comes to mind, but that's not a word she'd have known.

August 4   **Salt of the Earth**

On a sunny day in 1990, I climbed into a rusty iron cage on a giant steel winch at *Wieliczka* (vee-a-LEETCH-ka) near Cracow, Poland. A dust-covered red light went green and I hurtled down into the inky black of an ancient salt mine. For claustrophobes like me, freefalling for quarter of a mile in a cage the size of an iron maiden in the rattling dark is memorable, even if your hard hat wasn't crushing your head, which mine was. I went back 100 years as each dimly lit-level whizzed by. The dirt was inches from my face and I felt it get colder.

After an eternity, the cage jolted to a stop and it was 1500 CE, give or take. Freed from the iron maiden, the tour guide immediately told me to lick the wall. This I did (it was salty). Later, in the hotel bar, I wondered how many people licked the cave wall at that spot. Then I wondered how many people have ever licked a regular wall. Then I had more vodka. Tomorrow I reveal what I learned about Jesus, toilet paper, consumptives and decay 327 meters beneath the surface of the Earth.

August 5   **Wyborowa Dude**

As I strolled in an ancient salt mine, hundreds of feet beneath the surface of the Earth, I pondered how dangerous such places are and how claustrophobic I am. My employer, Seagram, the now defunct drinks company, had US distribution rights for a Polish vodka. Even Poles struggle to pronounce its name. I rounded-up some journalists, asked Seagram's owner if I could use one of his Gulfstream V jets and organized a press junket. Laudatory headlines, I was sure, would result. Sales and my career would skyrocket.

This was 1990. The Polish Communist government collapsed the year before and the Soviet Union would itself die the next year. Food was rationed. Poland was a nation on edge and my press boondoggle turned out to be a disaster.

For starters, there was no distillery and I tartly upbraided one of my guests – a big name food writer – for his ignorance of Polish current events. And nobody thought to mention the large domestic airport central to our schedule was closed for repairs. The corporate jet had a serious mechanical problem in flight and one imbroglio required the intervention of a Polish Air Force colonel who demanded US$500 before we could talk.

Oh, gosh, the mine. Our guide, lanky and 65, was a witty historian, spoke elegant English and was proud of his upcoming trip to America. "My mother told me to bring toilet paper," he noted dryly. "Her sister says, in the US, it's like sandpaper."

Wieliczka began around 1280. Every 100 years or so, the miners created elaborate religious sculptures out of salt, the Pieta, the birth of Christ and so forth, but mines are moist and drippy and there's a reason you don't make statues of salt. Time and water have taken a toll on the religious symbols – 1700s Baby Jesus, for example, now looks like a loaf of grey bread.

At the deepest level, there's a vast salt cathedral, a tribute to Poles' eternal spiritual devotion. Hundreds of single beds, each with a neatly folded red blanket, are where the pews should be. The Soviets "encouraged" heavy industry which fouled the nation's air for decades, making life worse for respiratory patients. Salt acts like an air filter, so many Poles spent months at a time healing in the cathedral's pristine space. Think about that the next time you pick up a saltshaker.

Author's Note: I'm sorry this piece ran so long. I didn't have time to write something shorter.

August 6 — **Every Man Should Have a Sport**

When I was 12 or so, my parents insisted I try out for a basketball team – this despite my never having held the orb in question and having shown not an atom of interest in eye-hand activities. At the gym, I ran up and down the court with the other boys, thinking well, gosh, this is simplistic. Suddenly we all stopped. The grim faced coach looked at me and said, "Take it out." I deduced it referred to the ball because he flung it at me.

"Take it out." I wondered at this for a long moment. "He can't mean leave the building, can he?" As the coach later told my mother, "John has no ball-handling skills, no concept of the game's rules and no sense of team sport. But it's ok, 'cause he's slow too".

Thus ended my career in sport, not counting the Debating Team, where eye-strain and paper cuts were an ever present danger, and a full day on the rowing team in England. Most of that day was spent in a pub.

August 7   **Pa**

I won't burden you with stories of my father, born over a hundred years ago today – his stunning heroism in WWII after a shaky start, how he turned around a gritty and corrupt business and ran it for 55 years, his belief in the better angels of our nature, an uneducated man who cherished education, the delight he took in being alive and his abject patience with an arrogant son.

He's pictured kitted out in 1923's very best golfing attire. Like me, he wouldn't have known which end of a golf club to hold.

My father now resides in the undiscovered country. He was the most wonderful man I've ever known.

Happy birthday, Pa.

August 8   A Facial

My brother, son and nephew can grow full beards much overnight. I've seen it happen. They do this largely to smite me; they're very Old Testament that way.

After months of not shaving, I only achieved what looks like Angry Homeless Guy beard. Spiky and patchy, Angry Homeless Guy beard does not even get near Hipster with Man Bun, Balding Midlife Crisis Guy or Horny Adjunct English Professor at the Local Community College beards.

I am in good general health. I don't live near a nuclear power plant, a Super Fund Site or Donald Trump's makeup artist. I don't watch too much porn, I get lots of rest and I hydrate. I'm appealing for suggestions – I'll do anything except move to Vermont or wear Crocs.

August 9   Boom, Sonic

One summer night, I boarded the Concorde for the Atlantic crossing. Though posh, privations occurred. It was a narrow body aircraft, closer to a rocket really, and, with constant service for three hours, getting to the loo was out of the question. Trollies in the one narrow aisle serving the best wines produced a lot of urine. Well of course the trollies didn't produce the urine and stop being a fussbudget.

Perhaps the most annoying feature was cigarettes. British Airways designated the left side of the plane smoking and the right nonsmoking. The cabin crew were bewildered by my complaint; lovely people, the British, but dotty.

The curvature of the Earth was as elegant as my table manners. BA gave each passenger an extravagant cashmere scarf emblazoned with CONCORDE to show how wonderful you were. I left mine in the cab on the ride home from Kennedy.

August 10 𝒪**ly Weekend Travel Kit**

Trilby by Lock & Co, a bespoke Brigg umbrella, week-ender bag from Tustings and the covert coat by Benson and Clegg (see September 16th).

August 11 𝒪**Actual Dialogue at Brunch**

My Friend: "God, you're such a pretentious snob."
Me: "Complete tommyrot," I reply, tartly fluffing my cravat.
MF: [Takes huge swallow of *mimosa*]
Me: [Polishes his *pince-nez*]

August 12 **Bang, Bang!**

Today England celebrates The Glorious Twelfth, an ancient tradition in which hunters and the manufacturers of bullets, shot, sights, calls, scents, bows, arrows, infrared

vision goggles, camo wear, duck blinds, drones, whistles, handheld GPS devices, electronics, video and other gear celebrate the animal kingdom by killing game birds. Americans are much more evolved. We just shoot each other and no special day is required.

August 13 — **Lower the Portcullis!**

In their obituary, The Telegraph wrote that Medieval historian Eric Christiansen "knew the dust of archives well, but his life was not dry as dust at all." A Fellow of New College, Oxford, he typified the worldly-wise post-war English scholar. There's abundant academic pursuit of things Medieval, but dons like Christiansen aren't in abundance.

Consider this sparkler from a 2015 issue of The New York Review of Books: "If New York is London", Christiansen argued, "then [the English County of] Kent is Connecticut".

It has been my lot to know each of these four locales well (Kent being both an English county and an artsy town in Connecticut). Three are beguiling, brimming with food, drink, laughter and intellectual, cultural and social life. The last has a grating superfluity of golf-playing white men in Beemers. Fie on them, their toothsome wives and overachieving children.

August 14 𝔗ime After Some 𝔗ime

During the blistering summer of 1928, my father, then 20 and still not old enough to vote, walked into a jewelry store on South Pearl Street in Albany and told the owner he knew how to repair watches – a remarkable claim from a young man who'd quite likely never held such a device in his life. Remarkably, they hired him. During his brief employ, he bought a gold Swiss-made wristwatch.

I wear that old timepiece often. Its Radium-coated hands and numbers glow green as if nothing happened.

Not Calvin Coolidge or the wars or the Depression or the Army or the Holocaust or JFK or the loves and deaths and starting over and babies and sweat and heartbreak, the laughter, nor the worry nor the whisky or the man on the moon.

August 15 𝔖tep Up to 𝔥ealth

With The Plague now in retreat, we can all take steps to maintain mental health, to live each day to the fullest, to enjoy life. For example, never again will I step on the bathroom scale because no good comes of self-absorbed behavior. The Lord gave us the gift of Big and Tall shops for a reason. Are we to deny our Lord and Savior? Another positive step I am taking as of today concerns beverage alcohol. I am no longer adding tonic to my breakfast gin and tonic, thus avoiding needless sugar and calories. What positive steps will you take today?

August 16 ## **From a Lepidopterist**

My friend insists some of the graceful insects that visit our summer gardens are misnamed. They should not be called butterflies, she claims, because the word makes absolutely no sense whatever. She argues for "flutterbies" because "that's what they do". Her logic is compelling. Butterflies have inhabited Earth for more than 56 million years.

August 17 ## **My Long Moment with Craig**

It's ungallant to dish about a man of renown who's also dead, but let's draw the curtain back this once, shall we? A fawning crowd of 300 or so Ladies Who Lunch filled the Four Seasons private dining room in Manhattan that day. I was the host of this Seagram-sponsored bacchanal honoring Craig Claiborne, the famous NYTs food writer and restaurant critic. Mr Claiborne wasn't drunk but he had been richly over-served, as had Julia Child who introduced him. His speech was jumbled and slurred, his audience worshipful.

The lunch and show now over, I escorted Mr C to the restaurant's 52nd Street entrance where a limo waited. We were attended by a gaggle of his chirping acolytes. As requested, I had two chilled bottles of Perrier Jouët and two champagne flutes placed in the Seagram limo "for the ride back to the Hamptons".

Mr Claiborne was Southern gentility itself. He placed a priestly-soft hand on my cheek where it lingered and he asked if I'd like to go along for the ride. My praise of his speech was fulsome in the precise meaning of the word. I effortlessly removed his hand from my face, wished him a *bon voyage*, and he, with the chauffeur as support, teetered into the blistering summer sun.

August 18 You Call That a Fish Fork?

The French have excellent cuisine. The English have excellent table manners.

August 19 More Wine, my Pet?

Dans l'Ecole Militaire, I encountered a plebe, a large, bright-eyed young man called Daniel Denton. One September, after the summer break, Cadet Denton eagerly discussed his summer job. He had spent two and a half months masturbating bulls, whilst wearing substantial rubber gloves. Most Cadets mowed lawns or, in one case, delivered beer.

August 20 — 𝕮rustacia 𝕴ondinium

A ten-minute walk from Half Moon Street in Central London is the exquisite Connaught Hotel. Newly arrived after a gritty East European junket, I settled-in and ordered lobster and a white *Burgundy* from room service and then slipped into a restorative bath. Room service proved faster than my ablutions.

From the reception room, the waiter, who'd made quick work of setting the table, asked cheerfully, "Shall I crack the lobster and serve you in the bath, Sir?" *Gosh*, I thought, *that fellow's sure devoted to his job.*

August 21 — *Allo, Allo?*

There's a charming French expression to describe an elegant claret, *Comme le petite Jesu en culottes de velour* (Like the baby Jesus in velvet pants). The phrase, common in Bordeaux, captures the silky richness of a properly-aged Margaux, for example.

If however you use it in, say, the commune of Cognac, as I did, where it is unknown, you'll embarrass yourself in the most exquisite way you ever have in your entire soggy life, as I did. Your French colleagues will take a sudden interest in their shoes. You will know what eternity feels like.

August 22   𝕿unnel Vision

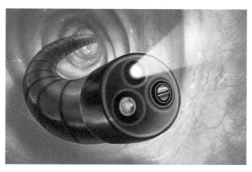

Last August I had a colonoscopy, a procedure known medically as "a hiney root canal". Once on the table, I decided to amuse the staff with my breezy insouciance.

I began to regale them with the history of peristalsis, the wavelike motion of the large intestines which moves waste southward.

"It was named for *Peracelsus Von Bastis von Hoenheim*, a student of *Mesmer*." I then added winningly, "Perhaps you'll find this doozy of an anecdote of interest. So one day – you're not going to believe this – *Herr von Hoenheim...*".

At this, the grim-faced nurse clapped an oxygen mask over my face with a speed, force and enthusiasm not consistent with good OR practice. "Breathe deep," she growled.

August 23   𝕭ondage

Count Robin de la Lanne-Mirrlees was a Scottish aristocrat whose life of wooing beautiful women and drinking fine wine was the basis for the character James Bond. In Ian Fleming's **On Her Majesty's Secret Service**, Bond's cover was that of a genealogical researcher Sir Hilary Bray.

De la Lanne-Mirrlees was in fact a heraldic genealogist for the College of Arms London. His full name was Robert

Evelyn Milne Stuart le Prince de la Lanne-Mirrlees. There was of course an actual James Bond too, an American ornithologist who knew Fleming. The next question please?

August 24 **Butteraceous**

Add: The above word to your wine vocabulary.

Use: When next you hoist that rich, oaky Chardonnay at wine snobs Fred and Linda's over-decorated center hall Colonial.

Do Not Use: To describe Fred and Linda's flirty and ridiculously hot 22-year-old daughter, home from Yale for the weekend.

August 25 **The Cockleshell Heros**

In the 1990s, I stayed for a time in the glamorous *Château Magnol* in the city of Bordeaux in southwest France for a wine-soaked romp in the warm sun of a French summer. A vast lawn rolls out behind the *château* and two grassy mounds – each 20 feet tall – are midway, surrounded by evergreen trees. During the war, the mansion was home to the Nazi admiral commanding U-boats in the region and the mounds were ammo storage units.

A team of British commandos, sent to destroy German submarines on an estuary of the *Fleuve Gironde*, were captured and imprisoned in those dank storehouses in 1943. The details are sketchy, but in the concrete, you can still see the machine gun bullets that took their lives after a call from Herr Hitler.

The mounds are so strong and intricate that, after the war, the French couldn't flatten them, so they just covered them with sod and went back to making wine.

"There is some corner of a foreign field that is Forever England", reads a bronze plaque.

August 26   ## A Commercial Traveler

Disrupting Manhattan's Park Avenue in a lunchtime parade of 32 restored 19th Century four-in-hands circa 1987. This Seagram PR effort made us deeply unpopular from CPW to 51st Street. Though quaffing Champagne, I'm gimlet-eyed as always.

August 27   ## To End All Wars

In 1928, 31 nations signed The Kellogg-Briand Pact rejecting war as a means of national policy. In the intervening 93 years, there have been no wars or armed conflicts on Earth, attesting to the immense success of this agreement which remains in full force and effect today.

August 28   **Wild Life**

Just as swallows come back to Capistrano in spring, every August Saratoga sees the return of the Northeastern Large-Breasted Bed Thrasher. The Thrashers are here again, blissfully ignoring The Plague. Noted for their piercing squawk, they're hugely popular in the foothills of the Adirondack Mountains. Unique plumage and repetitive beak movement, as if she were chewing gum, make the animal easy to identify.

Ornithologists are at a loss to explain the bird's large population in and near the taverns on Caroline Street, though the incessant thrum of ear-splitting sound systems may play a role. Some experts believe it's related to the seasonal concentration of the Rearward-Billed Knuckle Dragger, a gormless bird which tries to mate with the Thrasher and can be seen encouraging it to dance in a clumsy ritual.

In September, both animals roost in small sanctuaries with names like Oswego and Oneonta. There they spend fall and winter in filthy nests The State of New York jokingly calls dorm rooms.

August 29   **The Holy See**

The NYTs once described Saratoga Springs as the Vatican of horse racing. Our hats aren't as pointy, but we frequently wear special costumes and worship mammon just like they do. Like the College of Cardinals, our social scene is internecine and unforgiving. The faithful flock to both places in obeisance to the imaginary.

August 30   **Donkey Punch**

One lazy late summer afternoon, decamping from a vacation rental in Bearsville, NY, I punched a mule in the head because his teeth were sunk deep into the neck of a pony which was pulling a twee little red and white sulky occupied by two panic-stricken old people, the guy driving the thing and his wife seated next to him. If you've got a better opening sentence, I'd like to see it.

She picked up a cinder block and wanted to smash the mule in the face and her husband was seconds from infarction. He'd just had one two weeks prior.

After I punched it, the mule, now with murder in its eyes, chased me around a field for 20 minutes. Finally the mule's owner, a toothless harridan who did not observe normal routines of personal hygiene, arrived to heap bitter invective on me for upsetting her mule.

The cinder block was abandoned and neither the old man nor the pony died. After being chased by that beast, however, my thighs hurt so much, I wish I had.

August 31   **Home Bound**

On Sunday, August 31, 1997, I woke early to pack for my routine trip to London, but Diana's Paris car crash put a stop to that. Soon a sea of flowers, plush toys and notes spread out from the iron fences of Buckingham and St James's Palaces. The sea grew larger.

I lived then with my wife and children in the village of Newtown, Connecticut. Soon, in this rural place, flowers appeared round the giant flagpole that occupies the main intersection. Flowers for a dead English princess, in the middle of the New England countryside. The supermarket bouquets round our flagpole were haunting, but bigger tears still, borne of bigger heartbreak, awaited the people of Newtown.

September 1   Act Now!

My birthday falls on the fourth of this month and Asprey's have a jolly nice Champagne Cooler for £14,628.20, not including shipping, Champers or ice. My butler Finial's watery red eyes have glanced at the thing online more than once of late. It's more for him than me really; he is, you see, so very devoted to his profession. The cooler can make it to Saratoga in time if you get a wiggle on.

September 2   An Oliver Family Memory

I took this snap on this date in 1995, as my-then wife, Fiona Jean, escorted our son, Cucumberbatch, to his first day at the prestigious Wankerton School in the West Bonkage Fens. Each term's tuition was equal to the 2019 GDP of Liechtenstein, but I didn't mind since I believed he'd consort with the right sort of boys.

I was wrong. His time there was fraught because nobody could come to terms with his love of modern dance and

his devotion to the Wrestling Club. In the end, he graduated from Colonie Central High School, Colonie, NY, and is studying pre-veterinarian tech at Hudson Valley Community College. A happy outcome all round.

Of a summer day, Fiona Jean left me for a *bien pensant* boffin from Pitlochry.

I took little notice as I was much involved with a milkmaid on the estate who was great with child. Not mine however as it turned out. Saucy wench.

September 3 — The Importance of Being Oscar

"Twenty years of romance make a woman look like a ruin; but twenty years of marriage make her something like a public building."

— Oscar Wilde (1854 – 1900)

NOTE: The target of Wilde's joke is the institution of marriage, not the appearance of middle age women, *ie*, what happens to them when they put up with a man for decades.

September 4 — A Prognostication

When I was born on this date in 1953, my mother's physician, Dr Tobacco, grandly proclaimed I'd become either a priest or a prizefighter. Time proved him better at alliteration than prediction. As an adult, I encountered Dr T in a bar near his home on the Caribbean island of St John's – where he, though ancient, continued to practice medicine. Good physician, excellent taste in rum, devoted to his profession. After our boozy lunch, he returned to his office.

September 5   Scale

Yesterday, for my evening meal, I was piscivorous and now, funnily enough, the nice people at The Oxford English Dictionary have it as their Word of the Day. It means to dine on fish – in my case a superb sea bass accompanied by a bottle of Cakebread Chardonnay. I ate at 30 Lake, an elegant Saratoga eatery where my main course sparked an innocent but vital question, "What sea did this sea bass come from please?"

The bartender, two waiters, one assistant waiter, the chef, the sous chef, the hostess, the sommelier, a bar back, a busboy, the parking attendant and the couple seated at the table behind me were unable to answer the question. I expressed disappointment to the joint's charming owner, whilst complimenting her food, *carte des vins* and service. From the uniquely piquant flavour, I feel sure it was the *Sargasso*. The gyre there makes all the difference, as you know.

September 6   It's Chill

The Latin root of lachrymose (to cry) is tears (*lacrima*). In fact, the Italians make a wine called *Lacryma Christi*, the Tears of Christ – as featureless a fermented beverage as ever existed. I reckon Oenophile Jesus is weeping because

the wine that bears His name is so dull. You'd think somebody in His position could demand better adult beverages, say, a *Bâtard Montrachet* or Michelob ULTRA. Being a deity worshiped by 2.8 billion people isn't all that. Plus your parents are a lot.

September 7   Chess Then?

My PR group at Seagram once made presentations introducing ourselves to the new boss, a formidable South African. A Rhodes Scholar, Oxford grad, Harvard MBA, tall, elegant and saturnine, he was intimidating like you read about in books. The meeting ran late, so when my turn came, I began jovially with, "In the interest of time, I won't burden you with my checkered past...".

"Are you instead going to burden us with your checkered future, Mr Oliver?" he asked to guffaws.

September 8   God Save the Prince

In 1995, I met HRH Prince Philip aboard Her Majesty's Yacht Britannia. This was *sui generis* – a Latin expression meaning "Shit, that was weird." I had a backstage pass to RoyalLand and it wasn't all Pimm's Cup and strawberries. HRH's Private Secretary, Brigadier Sir Miles Hunt-Davis GCVO, CBE, with whom

I liaised, found your humble correspondent deeply revulsive. His grandeur was otherworldly *en haute, en bas.*

I concede my skills as Chief Protocol Officer to a gaggle of GE boffins were less than top hole. One such executive, a man of proud Irish roots, spent the afternoon on HMY flicking cigarette butts onto the adjacent yacht and my entreaties for him to stop failed. Further invitations to hang with the Buckingham Palace gang have been thin on the ground. I mention all this because some in England think a new Royal yacht would cheer the Plague-rattled peasants.

September 9   **Roll Out the**

My personal brand needs a reboot, a *soupçon* more gravitas, more zing. The Harvard MBAs who advise me decided to insert "The" between John and Oliver, in the manner of Robert The Bruce, William The Conqueror, Ivan The Terrible, Vlad The Impaler and Thomas The Tank Engine.

John The Oliver will grab market share in key demos, capture influencers' attention, increase audience excitement and grow differentiation from that HBO guy – along with other codswallop Marketing people say.

The rollout begins in 2023 and will include a new logo, graphic standards, user segmentation studies, themed tactical clothing, outdoor and print advertising and action figures. The entire team has worked hard to make this the most successful launch since New Coke. The Oliver Communications and Lawn and Garden Centre family of companies look forward to sharing more news in the exciting weeks ahead. Thanks for all you do.

John The Oliver

September 10

Smooth Talker

w/ President Dick Coffey

At 21, I hosted a TV show on the Albany PBS affiliate interviewing candidates for the New York State Legislature. One such was Assemblyman Clark Wemple. For three takes, I flawlessly recited to the camera a 40 second open, turned effortlessly to the guest and then, with gravitas beyond my years, said, "Wemple to the show, Mr Welcome".

On my third fumble, the director spoke to me sharpish like. I eventually learned television, but there were more Mr Welcomes in my future.

Seagram gave me a TV show too. It was better, but only marginally so.

September 11

Capitol Idea

When I was 21, I worked in The New York State Capitol in Albany. Inside it looks like an ancient castle owned by a crazed Romanian duke – dark, forbidding carved sandstone lit by dim bulbs. On the outside, the Capitol building is a *mélange* of three wildly different architectural styles. Don't ask.

My colleagues in the Legislative Bill Drafting

Commission were all Damon Runyon, including a defrocked priest, two enforcers for a bookie, a card sharp, an ex-Navy medical corpsman and a kid who did the best **BBC World Service** imitation you ever heard. I, an erstwhile beer truck driver, rounded out the group. You had to arrive early if you wanted a chair for the day. A tiny devil's head is carved into one of the ornamental stone railings adorning the place – a curse on NYS from a long ago Italian stonemason. This tells you all you need to know about my corrupt, noisy, fractious, wonderful and beloved State.

September 12   **⸫Alone of a ⸫uesday**

I never post this meager story on 9/11 because it's a solemn occasion. Here is my tale however, with all its solipsism, 20-plus years on.

I had lunch that day in London's financial district with a senior Hill & Knowlton executive at *Coq d'Argent*, a pricy restaurant just down the way from St Paul's. It operates in The City still. The hour and a half was businesslike.

We returned to a freakish scene in the consultancy's huge lobby in Bloomsbury. Hundreds of young people shrieked as giant TV screens showed mountains of black smoke billowing from the North Tower. As we stood there gaping, a plane plowed into the South Tower. What we saw next is unrepeatable and I muttered to no one in particular, "I hope the Americans don't do anything stupid".

The only American in that lobby, I was hustled to a subterranean conference room to watch this *Grande Guignol* and somebody brought me a biscuit and tea in a cup of fine china. Later as my colleague and I rode to deposit me at The Mayfair Hotel, his mobile rang. Neither tower had fallen, but The Financial Times wanted to know GE

Capital's reinsurance exposure to the towers' collapse (it was immense). I urged a deeply vulgar response which memory says was delivered, but one can't be sure. In the lounge that night, a drunk couple with American accents danced lovingly.

I hated them then. I hate them still.

September 13   **Republicans on Parade**

In 1969, President Nixon and his senior cabinet officers visited Pope Paul VI at the Vatican and a large group of diplomats and reporters joined. The American delegation waited in an elaborate anteroom before being presented to the Holy Father. The group included Nixon, Kissinger, Attorney General John Mitchell and Secretary of Defense Melvin Laird, a particularly awkward man. At last the moment arrived and a monsignor opened the gilded doors to the papal offices. "This way, gentlemen," he intoned. The tense Secretary of Defense had been smoking a cigar. Kissinger told Laird to get rid of it immediately.

Flustered, Laird jammed the lighted cigar into his suit coat pocket. The Pope greeted the Americans warmly and began a long speech in Italian. Soon, however, wisps of smoke began rising from Laird's coat. The hapless Secretary of Defense noticed and began slapping his pocket hoping to put the cigar out. Hearing the slaps, the large crowd concluded His Holiness said something warranting applause, so they did.

The bewildered Pope stopped mid-sentence, looked up from his speech and raised his eyebrows. Later Kissinger would tell this story, noting in his thick German accent, "It vas not our finest hour".

September 14   **Piece Be with You**

"Irenic" means to promote peace. If you're itchin' for an ancient Greek pun, you're in luck. "*Eirēnē pantessi, episkopos eipen epelthōn*". Irene was also the name of an eminent courtesan – so, depending on phrasing and tone, the expression means "Peace be to all, said the Bishop as he approached" or "Irene is for everybody, said the Bishop as he approached". Good night, Irene.

September 15   **Rendering unto Caesar**

My artful money-management skills have created a hellish *contretemps* with the United States government. I won't name the agency, but the initials are IRS. Long before The Plague, I ceased socializing, eschewed luxury goods and, most tragically, avoided the posh eateries and swank cafes that sustain a man of my sophistication. Cheap foods are so vulgar. Last night, for example, I dined in crepuscular gloom solely on CaviarHelper, a bowl of panko and some chicken lips. Two well-chilled bottles of 1979 Pol Roger cheered me, but not much.

September 16   **Umbra**

London's Swaine, Adeney and Brigg make umbrellas for the Royal family. I own one (an umbrella, not a Royal family). Because I have the habit of gracious living, my Brigg brolly is bespoke, a gift from the firm's managing director in exchange for a case of Crown Royal. As a Seagram executive, I could bestow such largess.

For 30 years, this incomparable device has kept me and companions various dry in cities, villages and in the countryside. I once thwarted a brigand with it, discouraged a rude canine and employed it numberless times to inflict conversation on the innocent. It has a wangee handle – not bamboo – and my name is inscribed on the brass collar. That same collar carries the symbol of Brigg's Royal Warrant from HRH Prince Charles. An inter-web journey will reveal how colossally expensive these items are (see August 10th).

September 17   # **Cap and Trade**

Among America's gifts to the world is the Baseball Cap. I am not given to displays of sartorial vulgarity, but bedhead is a personal struggle, so I occasionally wear one of two Baseball Caps. The first is emblazoned with *Devoucoux*, a *Biarritz* saddlery of infinite elegance.

The clouds in *Biarritz* are whiter than God's underpants and when it rains, it rains Perrier. The other, a royal blue number, shows in gold The Great Seal of the United States and the words Baghdad Diplomatic Support Service Iraq. Baseball is played in neither place so why Baseball Caps are required eludes me.

September 18 **Hunting of the Snark**

Chapel Hill, North Carolina, November 2016. The tie is the Oliver Hunting Tartan. What prey my Scots ancestors were hunting with those colours as camouflage is lost in the mist of time. For this we can all be grateful – and for the fact that I'm not wearing a kilt. I do not inflict my legs on a blameless citizenry, even in the South.

September 19 **Write Makes Right**

I make no secret of my love of all things tactical. Until today this just meant the Tactical Flashlight and my Tactical CIA-Approved Cargo Shorts. A newly-arrived email has me tingly with anticipation for the new Tactical Pen which I will order for $49.99 from All Things Tactical. It features a tactical, pressurized ink cartridge and a tactical knife.

I'll use this instrument, for example, to write a list of cold cuts I need at the grocery store, then use the knife to slice the turkey, ham and *sopressata*. I will also write tactical notes to my many enemies. If you've not wronged me, you have nothing to fear.

September 20   # Some Like it Cold

Les Américains sont nés avec un réfrigérateur dans leurs bouches – Americans are born with a refrigerator in their mouths – a French expression suggesting the American obsession with "ice cold" everything, especially their God awful, mass produced, undrinkable lager. When cold enough, you can't taste it which is a gift from the Universe.

September 21   # It's Time to Light the Lights

When my children were little, we often traveled the New York State Thruway between Westchester County and Albany to visit my father. In those years, the highway featured toll collectors in booths. At each of these, the little darlings demanded I sing the theme song from The Muppet Show to the long-suffering collectors. This I did – to the bewilderment of many, except for one fellow who joined me in song. The children were over the moon.

September 22   # This Business We Call Show

My first Big City gig was writing and directing a Public Service Announcement starring Dina Merrill, who died at 93 in 2017. An actress and heir to the vast EF Hutton fortune, she was married to actor Cliff Robertson. Ms Merrill was, in addition, extremely nearsighted, hugely self-conscious about it and famously impatient to boot. A TelePrompTer with a magnifier was secured for her convenience.

On the fourth take, the young cameraman shouted into his headset, "Hey, she's squinting A LOT!"

Dina Merrill [annoyed]: "Who said that?"
Me: "Just a tech miss, Ms Merrill. We'll fix it in post."
DM [angry]: "Fine. Tell that cameraman to keep his mouth shut."
Me [Shaky]: "Of course. Let's go again please?"
Me: [GULP.]

Dina and me at a celebrity tennis tournament in Houston, circa 1981.

September 23   **Homer**

My father's beer business, dusty and tiny, had a fleet of two trucks and, for 30 years, Red Huskie drove one of them. His real name wasn't Red Huskie; his real name was Homer J Something Unpronounceable in Polish. You didn't say it, he claimed, you sneezed it. Only 5' 7", Red was famous for his stunning capacity for drink, brute strength, precision beer truck loading and for having driven a pal's car into his girlfriend's living room one drunk night. All day, every day, shots and beers while delivering to Albany gin mills. Nights and weekends were for whiskey. Cigarettes every waking second and sweat poured off him on the coldest days.

I kidded him about his hands, which shook terribly. "That fuckin' coffee's bad for ya," he warned seriously. One gin mill had a 400-pound trapdoor to the cellar on the floor behind the bar and he was famous for being able to open the thing without help. After he tapped the kegs down there, Red climbed the cellar steps and pushed upward with his back, but the door wouldn't yield, so he pushed harder. The door and the morbidly obese bartender standing on it rose a foot in the air. Red and his friend, Tony, dreamed of their own portable shithouse business and schemed drunkenly for years. I visited his dirt floor apartment one night.

Staggering and nearly insensate, Red proudly handed me five worn notebooks. They were his poems. I should have said; I should have told you about his poems.

September 24   Me-OW!

I take pride in my foppish affectations, breathtaking pretensions and smug know-it-all-ism. Still, here's four things I learnt only on FB.

- The whole Schrödinger thing;
- The Overton Window;
- Dunning-Kruger Effect; and,
- That your cat is a fucking bore. I know Mittens/Sprinkles/Mr Wiggleton kept you going when Gary left and he's cute looking out the window at a bird or sitting in a box, but I'd rather listen to a whole Mike Pence speech right the way through. Get a dog for God's sake.

NOTE: The forgoing is a mere jocose provocation, so please don't rail, bleat or issue a *Fatwã*. I got three *Fatwãs* on me already.

September 25   Bon Appétit!

At Seagram, I hosted a swank Manhattan event which featured three food icons – James Beard, Julia Child and, from

The NYTs, Craig Claiborne. It was a Champagne-soaked evening with lots of celebrities and those who worshiped them. Mr Beard was gigantic and inert, whilst the other two guests of honour competed to be the more drunk. Such events, commonplace in my work, were complicated and fraught and I was relieved when they were over. Mr B is pictured looking dapper.

September 26   **Too Much Couth**

Soon after college, a scholarship sent me to Canterbury for grad school where a jolly "Welcome to England" dinner party was laid on for us foreign scholars. During this genteel black-tie affair, I used the innocent American word fanny, meaning buttocks. Jaws dropped immediately, utensils went to their plates and people took sudden interest in their shoes.

A Peer of the Realm seemed stricken, as if by a cardiovascular event or a speech by Jacob Rees-Mogg. In the country fewer than 24 hours, I had created an international incident. The host leaned over, paused for dramatic effect and whispered, "Well that means a bit of crumpet, doesn't it". This was not entirely edifying. In British English, fanny means vagina – a naughty vagina at that. When I tell you this was one of the more successful moments in my academic career there, I do not exaggerate.

September 27   **Webster's Defines...**

I started writing speeches at 25 or so. A greybeard, whom I quite liked, taught me sentence structure, pacing, how to keep the audience's attention and the like. In time, I learned The Blackberry Prayer too. That's the head-down position of nearly every audience member, typing on his or her Blackberry, while Mr or Ms Big delivered The Talk of their career.

It was said a speech should be like a beautiful woman's skirt – long enough to cover the basics, but short enough to maintain interest. Sexist twaddle doesn't cut it today, but it did circa 1980.

September 28   **BOJO**

I chatted with Boris de Pfeffel Johnson, at this writing the British Prime Minister, in a Cannes hotel lobby circa 2011. He was then London mayor. I said I enjoyed the speech he gave earlier in the day and noted I worked for GE. We have 330,000 employees, I said. "Oh, do you know Phil Winterbottom?" Bojo asked.

"No, I'm afraid not," was my witty reply. He then said nice things about General Electric, after which we parted.

September 29   **Car Talk**

When I was still a lad in high school, my father gave me a Triumph Spitfire, a car attractive to some young women of my acquaintance and to some young women with whom I hoped to become acquainted if you follow my meaning. Those familiar with the 1971 Spitfire know most every component of sexual congress is impossible to conduct within its confines. A strategic fellow, my father. Luckily I was a good tactician.

September 30   **Thanks for All You Do**

In linguistics, the word phatic means small talk or pleasantries. It can also mean a corporate meeting in which everyone is earnest, attentive and engaged, but no meaningful ideas are exchanged. Having attended more than one such confab, I hold phatic in high regard. Those still corporately employed are urged not to ponder phatic too deeply because no good can come of it. Now back to work, Wage Slave.

October 1   **Adventures in Journalism**

The refined American city of Savannah, Georgia, once boasted a significant Mob presence. After a wild party, a young man viciously beat a senior Capo's daughter. Two days later, he was found dead on the sidewalk in a good neighborhood with his genitalia in his coat pocket. The Savannah Morning News covered the murder and their headline read **Area Man Dies in Fall from Balcony**.

An aristocratic doyenne on her third Bourbon told me this in a voice all molasses and Spanish Moss. She said, "Mr Oliver, you need to understand, here in Savannah, we take care of *our own*". She lingered on the words our own. She lingered on them suggestively.

October 2   ## Word Choices

Whilst we're on the prickly subject of words, consider bumf. Largely British, bumf means bum fodder or toilet paper. The phrase describes the torrent of words – press releases, speeches, holding statements, talk points, strategy memos, Q&As, crises communications – which I and people like me write for corporate clients. The expression also suggests the appropriate use of such writing. Bumf.

October 3   ## Once in Edinburgh

A delightful tailor called MacTavish in a charming shop on The Royal Mile encouraged my giddy contemplation of the purchase of a kilt. His was a practiced art, but when he saw my legs he mentioned what in Scotland is call The Two Sock Solution. The wearer dons two knee socks on each leg to suggest musculature where nature has been deficient. In the end, cooler heads and my Scots penuriousness prevailed.

October 4 ## 𝕾t Patrick's Man

The man who owned Shaunessy's Towne Tavern in Albany, NY, brought balletic precision to bartending. I know this because I delivered beer to The Towne twice a week. With the sleeves of his starched white shirt rolled, his long white apron spotless and his head shaved, Jack Shaunessy at work was a thing of wonder. Not an atom was wasted and his every move – polishing a glass, pouring a shot – was pure connected grace. Not showy, just precise.

Jack got me a job in the NY Legislative Bill Drafting Commission, a kind of holding pen for Albany reprobates with connections. His obituary said he wanted to be remembered as a member of the public library. The elderly lawyers in three-piece suits who "breakfasted" at The Towne didn't notice Jack Shaunessy's precision. The regulars, drunk before lunch, didn't notice nor did the guy who brought the ice. But I did. I should have told him. I wish to hell I told him.

October 5 ## Wifey

In the glittering candlelight, a butler in red and gold hove into view holding a silver tray with five Champagne flutes, less than an arm's length from HRH Prince Philip, Duke of Edinburgh, Knight of the Most Noble Order of the Garter, Duke of Rothesay, Consort. He began to reach for a glass.

His spouse – at a remove of 20 feet – God's Holy Vessel on Earth, Her Britannic Majesty Elizabeth the Second, By the Grace of God of the United Kingdom of Britain and Northern Ireland and Her Other Realms and Territories, Defender of the Faith, Queen, saw him move.

She nearly, *but not quite*, raised an eyebrow in an act of negation so faint as to require an electron microscope to be seen. Philip slowly put his arm to his side and his expression did not change. Nor did hers. At dinner, each pat of butter is stamped with HM's coat of arms, so that's nice.

October 6   A Lake George October

In their 60 years in Lake George, NY, my relatives owned three big resorts, three restaurants, two bars and a book-shop. If you've been to that Village, you know the word "resort" is an imprecise term. These places featured wooden Adirondack chairs, each a gaudy green and each heavier than The Great Pyramid of Giza. They had arms you could land a plane on.

When I was eight, my cousin Vincent gutted a newly caught trout on just such a platform – his beer and ham sandwich undisturbed on the other arm. One sunny November Sunday, we played touch football just like a famous family of the time. A year later, in the TV room, we watched a dignified military funeral for the murdered leader of that family. For a little boy, it was magical.

October 7   ### Objet trouvé. Broadway, Saratoga Springs, NY, 2020

October 8   ### Ain't that America

In our time, beloved newspapers and periodicals have grown perilously thin or died. Where and how we read for leisure is transformed. It is in this context that I tell you **"Muzzleloader"** Magazine thrives – $6 at your local newsmonger for all your muzzle-loading needs.

October 9 — 𝒫erfidious Albany

Albany, NY, where I was born, is a down-at-the-heels political town. In the 1930s, four blue-collar locals tried something distinctly un-Albanian. They decided to steal a copy of Shakespeare's First Folio from the Williams College Library and sell it on the black market – a task for which they were especially ill-suited. To seem professorial, the gang leader dressed in a shabby, ill-fitting topcoat and it worked.

Their tale is dumb-head misadventure and oafishness – and it features a denouement with none other than Adolf Hitler. For more, buy **"The Shakespeare Thefts"** by Eric Rasmussen, St Martin's Press, 2012. When in Albany, stick to shots, beer and handing bags of cash to elected officials in parking garages.

October 10 — 𝒷linded by the light

If by some magic, you could see every movie ever made from the dawn of time to the end of the world and a day, **"The Blind Side"** would still be the worst piece of cinematic dog shit ever created. Last evening, had I owned a handgun, I would have shot the television to put it out of its misery.

When the viewer can see a car wreck nine minutes in advance of the script, your mission as a moviemaker has failed. When, in the second half of the film, you reuse clichés you used in the first half, your choice of profession is gravely defective. When an actor's performance is so wooden as to be a fire hazard, show business may not be the career for you.

October 11   # cA Day at the Office

One day at Yannas's Tavern, old man Yannas was on the sidewalk in the rain waiting for me and my beer truck. "Ya gotta get that fuckin' leaker [leaking keg of beer] outta the cellar. It's flatter 'n Kelsey's nuts." In those days, a half keg weighed about 260 lbs. Getting a leaker out of a cellar with a 20 foot drop alone was Sisyphean. Above is a glamour shot of a truck in my father's fleet.

October 12   # We Have Liftoff

I got this understated little number from the NASA online gift shop. I would have gotten the whole outfit, but they were right out of space suits in my size – Astronaut Porcine.

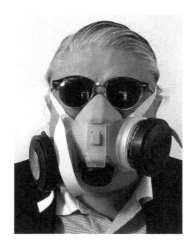

October 13   A Man in Full

I met writer Tom Wolfe on a Manhattan street corner and much earlier, at Chatham University in Pittsburg. He wore three different white suits that long ago day, but his shirt collars were a thing of Victorian wonder. I marvel at them still, so many decades on. He was, on both occasions, the quintessence of Southern gentility and manners.

October 14   How I Live Now

For my part, in the bright autumn gleaming before us fecund with promise, no longer will I consume Lucky Peking fried pork dumplings directly out of the newly-arrived carton with a spork wearing only cotton socks in the study.

[Editor's Note: We feel sure Mr Oliver means to say that he, and not the spork, is wearing the cotton socks. In fairness, he did have a lengthy luncheon today. Because of his lusty rendition of *Lady of Spain* in the lobby of HQ, some staff uncharitably suggested he'd been over-served. We countenance no such tommyrot here at Oliver Communications, Certified SpaPools© Dealer.]

Furthermore, whilst striding about my tonsured greensward, which is cared for by our well-muscled pool boy, Raoul, to whom my beloved wife, Fiona Jean, is so unfailingly considerate, my dressing gown will be consistently cinched. Complaints from passersby and staff are duly noted. Finally, on occasions where I find myself quite alone, and I fart vigorously, I shall say, "Excuse me", for that is what a gentleman does. Raoul is happy about these improvements, though he can be quite the slippery eel about such things.

October 15   Yaz

At Seagram, I had the bright idea to use Boston Red Sox icon Carl Yaztrzemski to promote a new light whiskey concoction (*Low Calories – Same Great Taste!*). I snagged one of the company's Gulfstream Vs and off we flew to media interviews in New England and Upstate New York.

In response to my brilliant PR effort, The Boston Globe penned a searing editorial bashing Seagram and the retired ballplayer for his post-career choices. Mr Y's a serious fellow in the best of times. These were not the best of times.

October 16   The Return!

"Do bring up a jeroboam of Pimm's Cup from the wine cellar like a good fellow, would you?" – me just now issuing instructions to my longtime butler, Finial, who is lately returned to Chateau Oliver. My barrister at Lay, Bakke and Wacket, London, Alfred Dingle-Foote, was insistent on an order of protection against Finial's wife, Siobhan, who's given to emotional upset. This I got. Finial is irascible, true, but his bride is termagant and no respecter of one's station.

October 17   The Oliver Manhattan Cocktail

Combine four (or 12) oz of Crown Royal Whisky, two dashes (or 18) of sweet vermouth and 12 (or 36) dashes of aromatic bitters. Pour into a cocktail shaker (or Tupperware bowl) full of ice cubes. Shake vigorously for 23 (or 23) seconds (the shaker, not you). Pour into a crystal rock glass of superior quality (or a Big Gulp cup from 7-11). Cut a substantial slice of fresh orange. Squeeze the juice into the rock glass (or Big Gulp), then gently drop the

orange slice into the glass (or Big Gulp). Drink and converse wittily.

Your only role, as always, is to drink and converse wittily; your trusted butler does the drink-making. For the wittiest exchanges, I find it helpful to have someone else in the room with you. Not an absolute requirement, of course.

October 18   # Rough Trade

The Russian Army is justifiably famous for its animalistic brutality. Consider this.

Near the end of World War II, a German regiment surrendered to two American soldiers – my father and his buddy, both sergeants. The Nazi commander, a major, was spotlessly kitted-out, gleaming and creased.

He seemed, my father noted, to be ready for a parade, the war's devastation notwithstanding. The German and his men surrendered, not because of my father's formidable skills as a warrior, but because they so ardently didn't want to be taken by Russians. Even Nazis feared them. Debates will ensue as to the brutality the troops of various nations, but the above anecdote tells a tale.

October 19 St James's, London

Pictured is my beloved Jermyn Street cheesemonger; I miss them and their Stilton every day. A few doors down are the best shirt makers on the planet, then Cuban cigars (Dunhill or Foxes). Across the way, on St James's Street, Berry Bros & Rudd for whisky. Nearby, in the Piccadilly Arcade, are Benson & Clegg, creators of my suits and Swaine, Adney and Brigg for my bespoke umbrella. You read that sentence correctly. For me, it's The Happiest Place on Earth.

October 20 A Sweet Course Perhaps?

For dessert, a swank Saratoga restaurant once offered "Signature Homemade Cotton Candy". Why such a thing required a signature I'll never know. And have you ever been at somebody's house where they made cotton candy (chiefly British: candy floss)? Me neither.

But you're thinking, Gosh, John, what dessert wine should I pair with my hot steaming bowl of cotton candy? A glass of *d'Yquem*? Not sugary enough. Vidal Ice Wine *avec* Splenda could work. *Tokaji*? Nah – might compete.

In the end, I went with a Late Bottled Chateau Sucrose from Rensselaer County, NY. Glycemic Today magazine gave it three syringes up. The wine's subtle notes of Froot Loops were the perfect accompaniment to the pink confection before me.

The ER doctor later that night promised my hallucinations would stop soon.

October 21 # OINK!!!!

Male pigs have orgasms that can last up to 90 minutes. It's as if God says, "Look, Pig, I got awful news about your life, with a bit of happy news now and again. You better sit down".

October 22 # Et Pourquoi Pas?

I had dinner years ago with a reporter friend in what was then Philadelphia's best restaurant, *Le Bec-Fin*. Told I was in the Seagram wine group, the sommelier said, "You must let me choose your starter". He gave us a bottle of *Chateau d'Yquem* and a huge portion of *foie gras*. It was transcendent. Weird, but true.

October 23 # Beware of the Dad

When my children were little, a terrible old harridan and her vicious dog lived near us. One snowy morning, as the children and I headed out across our garden to the garage, the dog appeared out of nowhere. He was right in front of my kids, growling ominously. I was at a remove from the children, who were now frozen with fear.

It's important to say I have utterly no eye-hand

coordination. None. And I have the visual acuity of a 90-year-old. I quick made a snowball which was flung at the mutt fortissimo. The icy projectile hit that effin animal right between the eyes – it hit him so hard, he stumbled backwards. The children, the mean dog and I all stood stock-still, each of us stunned by this impossible conquest. We stared at one another for a long moment, then the dog decamped at the quick march and the children smiled at their father. The End.

October 24   **Spy vs Spy**

In the intelligence business, it's axiomatic that Americans play checkers and Russians play chess. If you look at the way they toy with the US, Russians clearly play chess on five levels at once. Staying with the metaphor, you'd have to say British spies play snooker and, since no one on Planet Earth understands snooker, it shows just how cunning those people really are. The British table game incorporates autoerotic elements, too, as can be seen below.

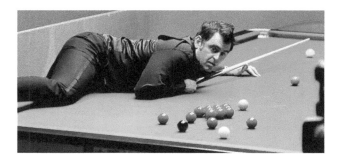

October 25   **Remember**

My father's US Army unit, the 45th Infantry Division, liberated a concentration camp close to the end of WW II. First, they shot all the guard dogs – because they were rabid. Next they arrested any inmate who looked the least bit healthy. Those were the Nazi guards. They shot them too.

October 26   **The Skinny**

I bought some ascots (cravats) a few months ago, a dated and affected form of neckwear. I wanted to resemble a refined *flâneur* of indeterminate age, perhaps the scion of a wealthy family of Belgian industrialists. What I got was Christopher Walken's creepy weirdo from Saturday Night Live. I mention this because a young ESPN sportscaster wore an ascot on TV this very evening. True, he's 29, Hollywood handsome and built like a Greek god, but still...

Mine hide a couple of my chins.

October 27 **Police: Woman Arrested After Injuring Female with a Glass Cup at a Pool Hall**

Saratoga is an oasis of sophistication, leisure and grace. Come for the culture, stay for the foxy-boxing.

October 28 **Education of the Secondary Kind**

Most of the concepts presented to me in high school proved – let's be generous – elusive. My core competency was "not applying" myself, a strength not highly regarded at *l'Ecole Militaire*. Entropy, nature's strong predilection for chaos, is a good example. My grasp of entropy was enriched, however, the instant I bought my first house, at 151 Palmer Avenue, Sleepy Hollow, New York.

Though I am a manly man, the word handy has never described me. For example, I once taught my 11-year-old son how to open the front door with a credit card because

I couldn't divine how to fix the knob/lock device. Anywhoo, I did at long last work out how to repair stuff around the house. You hire someone. Duh.

October 29 cA Moment for Reflection

These days here in the foothills of the Adirondack Mountains, natural warmth is elusive, sometimes only a memory. But not today. Today, the Sun gives you a little hug that whispers everything's OK. Today, here in the warm sunlight in the foothills of the Adirondacks, things are OK. The photo is by Gail Carmichael Stein, a Saratoga Springs artist and photographer of real accomplishment.

October 30 Ink-a-Dink-a-Don't

A tattooing emporium has opened mere steps from my abode. I'm not a fan of this mania afflicting my fellow citizens. Still, I did pause at the shop window. A tattoo is a chance to display ones rebel nature and this I would certainly like to do. Perhaps some multicoloured neck ink, I thought – *"Tippy Canoe and Tyler Too"*, or maybe *"Remember the Maine"* on my capacious behind? Nah. I'm going to stick with my nipple rings.

October 31 Era Era

A study by Southern Methodist University has determined the American state with the most psychopaths. To those

of us who lived and worked there for extended periods, the winner comes as no surprise. We could have told the nice people at SMU.

It is, ladies and gentlemen, The Land of Steady Habits, yes, The Nutmeg State: Connecticut, whose residents are called Connecticutters. The state motto is – and this is true – *He Who is Transplanted Still is a Nutmeg Bag*. The state seal is adorned with three grape vines because Connecticut is rightly famous for its wines (Chateau Bridgeport comes to mind). Perhaps it's the rich people and their golf or maybe it's the proximity to Rhode Island.

November 1   𝕳erd Not Seen

In 2000, a British PR consultancy gave me a great huge sheep's crook to symbolize something or other. Jetting about Europe on that junket, my rod and staff was the subject of ribald remarks, smutty innuendo and sexual hilarity on the part of cabin crews of no less than three national airlines. It was a jolly prop involving Little Bo Peep in highly unladylike positions. Cabin crews can be quite inventive, especially the Hungarians.

At long last, boarding a London plane bound for New York, a senior American Airlines flight attendant sees the crook as I take my seat. She heads my way double time, stone-faced, purposeful and full of the potent authority of her high office.

Through clenched teeth, she sputtered in near fury, "There's no room for that ... *thing* ... in first class, Sir."

"Oh, dear. *Where would you like it?*" I asked brightly, lingering on the words.

Some passengers giggled at this mild jape, but the doughty senior American Airlines flight attendant did not and the crossing was a chilly one for yours truly.

November 2

Government Versus Good Grooming

Last Friday, at Albany Airport, in a stunning example of governmental overreach, a Federal agent relieved me of my hair *mousse*. I patiently explained the importance of Product to a person with rich, lustrous and thick locks like mine.

The bald G-Man remained deaf to my entreaties, even after I told him who I was.

I launched into a spirited diatribe on the failures of government – and said I was sorry he was bald. As the police gathered, he muttered something about air safety, terroristic threats and jail time, but it was hard to hear over the hoots of derision visited upon him by my fellow travelers. *Sans* my *mousse*, my weekend in the nation's Capitol was in disarray – just like my coiffeur.

November 3

Foundering Founder

Americans aren't generally aware how close George Washington came to losing his job commanding the American forces. His principle talent seemed to be retreating or sneaking away in the dead of night. General Horatio Gates's big score at Saratoga – while GW hung out in Pennsylvania – didn't help. A conspiracy against the Army's leader festered in Congress and among senior officers.

It was called The Conway Cabal and, when it was all over, Major General Thomas Conway resigned his Continental Army commission and Gates issued a florid apology. Just think, our Capitol could have been Conway, DC, and the Father of Our Nation a guy named Tom.

November 4   # The Vicissitudes of Commerce

Me in St Petersburg protecting Mother Russia circa 1998. GE Capital looked at buying a big bank there, but due diligence revealed four board directors were convicted felons.

November 5   The Lady of the Avenue

The thing about my Aunt Marion was not her hunchback. She lived her small cloth coat life in a two-room apartment on Albany's Central Avenue with her husband, Chuck, a roofer who talked like Popeye. My father called her Auntie Mame and Little Sister of the Poor. When we put her in an old age home, she couldn't sleep because it wasn't loud like "the Avenue" – and because they took her "physic" away when she was admitted.

No, the thing about Aunt Marion was tea and Woolworths, which she loved in equal measure. With my tea just now, I time traveled to their dusty little parlor and Chuck asking, "Where's me cigarettes?" "Here you go, Chuck," she'd chirp with a smile that was luminous.

November 6   Roi Rage

I once saw a painting – on black velvet – of Elvis and Jesus called The Kings. The photo doesn't properly convey the transcendent, ethereal beauty of this masterpiece. I wanted the thing immediately, but my then-new wife counseled otherwise.

November 7   Political Panties

If you're like me – and thank sweet wriggly little Baby Jesus you're not – you've wondered which American president owned the most trousers while in office. Was it *fashionista* Dwight "Ike" Eisenhower, Bad Boy Haberdasher Harry

Truman or Peeping Tom James K "Peeper" Polk? Well, it's none of them.

It was Chester A Arthur and he had 80 pairs. One guy however who had relatively few trousers, but couldn't keep it in any of 'em, was Grover Cleveland. He had at least one child out of wedlock. When he took office, people shouted, "Ma, Ma where's my Pa?" Cleveland's supporters would respond, "Gone to the White House, ha, ha, ha".

November 8   **The Escaped Cock**

A pal in England who's related to DH Lawrence learnt of my deep scholarship concerning that writer. She asked for commentary which I was only too happy to supply. My experience with DH is now 40+ years old – and I wasn't much good at it then, but I recall five things clearly.

1. His poetry is near unreadable;
2. We spent a lot of time wondering if he wrote the same novel over and over;
3. DHL's muse and significant other, Frieda von Richthofen Weekley, had a rough go of it;
4. He was really horny most of the time and;
5. Your cat is a bore.

These insights may, of course, be 100% incorrect, apart from item 5.

November 9   **Elba Room**

There was a *contretemps* among my dinner companions last evening concerning the *mille–feuille*, a pastry known also as a Napoleon. A man seated to my left, previously thought by me educated, insisted the sweet was named for the Little Corporal – or, more dizzyingly, his nephew, Emperor Napoleon III.

This effrontery nearly subdued my *sang-froid*. The Napoleon is named after the City of Naples, as even feeble research will reveal. After some adroit wordplay, and with the Port gone, I gently bid us part and we did. But the damage lingered.

November 10   **Oh my God**

Some Christians chafe at being mocked, however real or fictive their concerns may be. Such people know little or nothing about Jainism, Hinduism, Judaism, little or nothing about Sikhs, Juche ideology, Deism, Buddhism, Baha'i, Shinto or Islam. Or atheism for that matter. They regard such beliefs as inferior which is part of being a good Christian. One does not object to religion, one objects to ignorance.

November 11   **Sunday Will Never be the Same**

One long ago Sunday, in a gleaming American supermarket, I plopped a corpulent **NYT**s down on the checkout conveyor belt. As the paper moved toward him, the cashier solemnly intoned, "The price of the paper went up today".

"Oh I know," I joked. "They're using bigger words."

He turned to the cashier in the next aisle with complete sincerity and said, "The Times price went up 'cause they're usin' bigger words".

November 12   A Love that Dare Not Speak its Name

I wish to discuss a delicate topic, one that may make some readers uncomfortable. The behavior I describe is deeply rewarding in physical pleasure for millions. It is usually done alone, often with a willing part- ner and sometimes in a group, though this is rare. To be direct, one inserts an object into a body cavity and then wiggles it around.

I speak of course of Q-Tips in the ear canal. The young are warned against this delightful pastime, suggesting dire consequences that have never happened to anybody ever. A RN of my acquaintance becomes agitated on the point, shouting *Cryptosporidium* over and over. This is not easy to do. Try it yourself.

Adults engage in this harmless rooting at will, but given America's Puritan roots, it is never mentioned in polite society. Unilever's Q-Tips Cotton Swabs are the market leader, racking up sales of some US$13 billion interna- tionally in 2015, the most recently available public figures*. They come in convenient packages of 7,000 Tips each.

The company says their Tips (or "swabs") can be used for "first aid and electronics". In a world where keyboard flesh wounds are a daily occurrence, Q-Tips are vital. Lastly, with tongue firmly in cheek, Unilever's PR team admonishes customers to never, ever put swabs in their ears. Put them in other people's ears, they advise.

* I made this up.

November 13   Make Love to the Lens

I've found the perfect job for my Golden Years. I'm going to be a plus-size male model. Jerry Adipose, SVP for IMG Modeling's new Brawny division, says he too has size issues. "I'm beefy, stocky – you choose the buzzword."

Mr Adipose, who may be my new boss, seems unclear as to the meaning of buzzword. For me, I'd go with husky, portly, regal, cuddly, chubette, big-boned, corpulent, fleshy, mildly obese, flabiddy or lumpen. While I await Jerry's call, how do you get onion dip off a keyboard?

November 14   Supply Chain Management

Estimable pal James writes, "Gosh, John, you're so worldly and sophisticated, how do you manage your CVS coupons?" Great question, James, and a critical topic.

When buying anything at CVS, the register will puke up a list of coupons longer than Interstate Route 95. There are real values on that paper – special hemorrhoid salves and earwax removers are good examples. Take the coupons home, read them thoroughly and carefully mark the ones you're likely to use.

Store the list in a safe, dry place no cooler than 63 degrees Fahrenheit. When you return to the safe, dry place in 30 days, you will see each CVS coupon has expired.

You then – and this is important – crumple the paper into a small ball and throw it away in the proper receptacle. Follow these steps carefully to get the most value from your CVS shopping experience. Good luck, James!

November 15 **ℋRH**

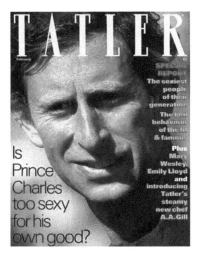

Happy birthday to Charles Philip Arthur George Windsor, Prince of Wales, Duke of Cornwall, Duke of Rothesay and Lord of the Isles. He's written and spoken cogently on art, architecture, horticulture, conservation, climate change, tampons and much else besides.

As for being too sexy for his own good, I feel his pain. But this man who would be king is a good, thoughtful man.

[NOTE: Today is not HRH's birthday – yesterday was. The Oliver Communications and Certified Propane Gas Distributor staffer who committed *haec lapsus calami* has been disciplined. Unfortunately, she likes that sort of thing.]

November 16 **𝒥hursdays at 9 ℰastern, 8 𝒞entral, on ABC**

A doctor threaded a TV camera up my nose and down my throat today in front of a live studio audience (two nurses and an intern). This was not as sexually alluring as it sounds and there's no ratings numbers till the Nielsen Book comes out next week. Ray Romano produced the pilot in which Kevin James plays my wacky but lovable neighbor, a Queens-based UPS driver.

TV icon Betty White plays his wacky but lovable great aunt who's always cracking wise with the *double entrendres*. The late Jerry Stiller plays their wacky but lovable, well, you get the idea. The lead character is Dr Sarah Sheinberg, a wacky but lovable Saratoga otorhinolaryngologist who doesn't accept my medical insurance or my romantic advances. "Date – with ME? You don't have a mucosa's chance in hell," she deadpans. [PLAY LAUGH TRACK]

November 17   **Gridiron**

"Life is my college. May I graduate well, and earn some honors."
                    Alum

The high school I attended was a rigorously military one. The Corps of Cadets shouted this imprecation when, in a football match, the opposition had possession,

"Repulse them! Repulse them! Make them relinquish the ball!"

The coach's famous admonition, Aim Low and Score, was employed by many cadets in a manner he did not intend. I always brought a book and a flask to such gladiatorial events for reasons abundantly obvious to any civilized person.

November 18   **Tennis No One?**

My college girlfriend's parents were inveterate tennis players, her father especially. He urgently wanted to teach me how to play. I explained I have no eye-hand coordination, no physical finesse, no speed – and no interest.

He was insistent, however, so of a summer evening to the tennis courts we wended. He explained the rudiments, how to hold the racket and such like. After 10 minutes of me flailing about, he declared the night too hot and humid and would I like to get some beers. I very much liked. We never spoke of the game again.

November 19   **Word for Word**

Even when little, I loved words, their sound, their meaning, their essence. But I detest some for the same reasons. Here are five.

1. Fingerling – yarn, potato or fish. Also an inappropriate medical exam. "Doctor Buxbaum, finger-lingering is unwelcome."
2. Muck. Nasty imagery, such as cleaning a horse stall (which I've done a lot) or muckrakers (who fight political corruption – I'm from Albany). In John Bunyan's Pilgrim's Progress, "the Man with the Muck-rake" forgoes salvation to concentrate on filth.
3. Nub or nubbin. Not to be confused with the supernumerary nipple. (Stop shrieking. You're scaring the dog)
4. Sleet. Not to be confused with more noble precipitations, like "mixed".

5. Sphincter. Your body has more than 60, so why do you only think about the one? What's wrong with you? Get help, Perv.

November 20 — *Arbeit Macht Frei*

As part of a press trip, I took some American journalists to Auschwitz in 1990, five of whom were Jewish. It was crushing beyond imagination. The tour was made more nightmarish by the behaviour of the docent.

In his hour and a half, he made eye contact with us not at all – preferring to gaze at the ground the entire time. He answered questions forthrightly in heavily accented English, his responses were detailed, he adjusted his glasses – and his eyes continued to examine his shoes.

He could have of course been on the spectrum for Autism or he could have been unable to look at what humans did to other humans.

November 21 — *Scarpe Rosse, Taglia 45, Prego*

Airline magazines are helpful if, for instance, you need a lavish dinner in a castle in Zagreb, which is also Danny DeVito's favorite eatery in that town. Today's example, from American Way magazine, is a Roman tailor who supplies vestments, pointy hats and other raiment to the Pope.

So you crave the same white socks as Francis? Just pop into *Ditta Annibale Gammarelli SNC, Via S Charia*

34, *Roma*, and stroll out with blessed footwear in your Skechers. To see if papal threads are right for you, take this simple test: do you like your friends to kiss your class ring while you bless them in Latin? If so, you know what to do, Your Holiness.

November 22   **Napkins on Lapkins!**

I possess eccentricities. I have, for example, more than once left a restaurant with the napkin (or serviette) stilled tucked firmly in my waistband. Yesterday, *après* brunch, I thusly strolled the byways of posh Saratoga, my odd accessory aflutter. The situation was only righted by shouts and gestures from a passing motorist.

At GE, I once lunched with a stunningly glamorous co-worker on whom I had a more than ordinary crush. A senior Washington operative, she was a serious intellect, Ivy-educated, Jennifer Lawrence look-alike and laughably out of my league. In the elevator back to our offices, I was charmed when she twice glanced at my crotch – lustily, I concluded. There's of course no way to discreetly remove a large white napkin from ones trousers in an elevator. Trust me.

November 23   ***Me OOOW!***

The gifts I gave my wife, The Hon Leesa Perazzo, for her birthday included two blouses from Hawes & Curtis, London. I call your attention to the description of the first item.

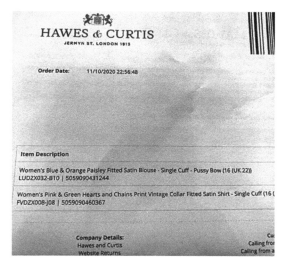

November 24   ***You Want to Put What Where?***

Customers in Paris supermarkets once rioted – stomped on each other actually – to get their Gauloise-stained fingers on extremely low-priced Nutella. Looking at the mad scene in one store, a weary *gendarme* noted, "It's like a crazy orgy".

A worldly sophisticate such as myself has of course attended many Parisian orgies. These are sparkling affairs, the participants witty and charming, the tenor piquant, the raiment inventive and the *obiter dicta* elegant. None of these occasions, in my experience, included Nutella however. Condiments, foods, beverages, flora, fauna and stimulants, yes. Sardine paste offered so many dizzying applications!

November 25 **Will that Be All, Sir?**

A great, though doddering, Victorian jewel of men's retail was London's New and Lingwood, founded in 1865. Elizabeth New and Samuel Lingwood's little enterprise thrived and they married. In my time, the Jermyn Street staff were to a man avuncular. They helped, but quietly, gently. The clothes, shoes and accessories were of the highest quality. It wasn't just a shop, it was an anchor in a roiling sea.

In the Piccadilly Arcade, N&L was as eccentric as you'd hope – posh but not meretricious. Shirts were £80 and worth every pence. N&L are now, alas, beset by modernity. They are An Important Brand, you see, with a gleaming "store" in midtown Manhattan and segmentation studies. The prices are vertiginous; the salespeople are hipsters. The London staff I knew, their kindnesses, their gentility, their grace, went away too soon.

November 26 **I Regret the Confusion**

Today I described the owner of **The New York Post**, **The WSJ**, **Fox News**, **The Times of London**, etc, as an "asshole". I apologize for this inappropriate word choice – it was rude and thoughtless. I should have said "dipshit".

November 27 **Imagine**

If I were vastly rich, I'd rent a swank ballroom and invite 5,000 of my closest pals for Champagne, good clarets, a posh dinner and dancing. Because I'm Bill Gates-wealthy, airfare, hotels and transfers are on me. You pay only for your minibar, dry cleaning, bribes, narcotics and bail money. The draw would be I will not make a speech, but I will validate parking.

November 28 **Them's Fightin' Words**

Facebook was invented so you can fight with strangers.

Marriage was invented so you don't have to fight with strangers.

Existence was invented so you can fight with yourself.

Work was invented because Gary from Accounting is an asshole.

Also, let's find out where Gary buys his shirts and burn that place down.

November 29 **Excelsior!**

New York State, where I live, was once the site of our nation's capital, has always been the Republic's money center and our governors (John Jay, DeWitt Clinton, Martin Van Buren, William Seward, the Roosevelts and Nelson Rockefeller) were rock stars.

New York State has two sections,

The City and Upstate. If you've lived here, you know Upstate is anything north of 97th Street in Manhattan.

Upstaters are angry because they live in an unforgiving hell-scape called Upstate. It's populated by feral gangs of roofers, lobbyists, clerks, lawyers, welders, meth dealers and homemakers. Any NY governor, regardless of party, is guilty for their poor life choices, grim jobs, halitosis and blotchy skin. Upstaters don't need to study or have facts to hate our chief executive. For them it's hereditary, like diabetes, gum disease and moderate to morbid obesity which they also have. My favorite governor was George Pataki because his last name is fun to say. (Letterman claimed his wife's called Jackie)

Our 54th leader, Elliot Spitzer, pictured, resigned when he got caught in a prostitution scandal based on a law he created.

November 30   **Oeufs**

The French word for eggs is the same sound I make when I trip on the sidewalk.

December 1   **English Cop, Foreign Bloke**

There was this fat, gray-haired bobby in Canterbury – and brusque doesn't capture him. He didn't like the idea of foreign me in Olde Blighty one bit. Still, he put me in the Resident Alien Book good and proper. Stamps, photo, fingerprints, passport number, the lot. At the end of our unpleasant 30 minutes together, he muttered, Get Out. I wasn't sure if he meant his poorly-lighted police station or his country or both. Probably both. Soon enough, out I got, leaving Kentish hops, apples, cherries and English roses behind. The Canterbury Police Station is pictured.

December 2 **1977**

Where I was the moment my mother died doesn't matter – maybe over Iceland, a good location given what I thought of her. In America, my father went to the hospital alone and said goodbye in the inexpressible dark December morning.

He then drove his red Cadillac back to his silent house, The Pink Palace, his children and grandchildren scattered long ago, the above ground pool long ago packed away and the drums and the upright player piano dormant.

Exhausted by her cigarette death, he did the laundry. A few days later, I asked why clothes got washed at 3 o'clock on a Tuesday morning. "Because they needed to," he said evenly.

And 82 Osborne Road just sits there as if nothing ever happened.

December 3 **Booty Gig**

A pricey women's shop here in Saratoga Springs features a product called Booty Booster, padded panties for ladies who feel their *glutei* are insufficiently *maximus*. Sizes run from Sm to 3XXX. The package proclaims in big letters, "Makes You Feel Sex!" This may not be true on account of it being a typo because there's no way I can figure how a couple of pieces of thick foam can do that. If Booty Booster did make you feel sex, it would be way more expensive, like Saratoga escorts.

December 4   **RMR'S BD!**

Today is Rainier Marie Rilke's birthday, so this morning I seduced an aristocrat under a Linden tree in his honour. Do you have any idea how hard it is to find an aristocrat and a Linden tree in Saratoga Springs, NY? RMR described a caged lioness thusly, "She moves the way clocks move".

December 5   **Please Make a Note of It**

After a totally unnecessary emergency session with my court-appointed psychiatrist, who, I got to say, seems pretty agitated lately, you shall hear from me no more concerning "**The Blind Side**", except to say I hate that movie with the white-hot heat of 10 million suns and wish nothing but ill on anyone associated with it. And, yes, Warner Bros Pictures, Alcon Entertainment and their heirs and assigns, I understand what "cease and desist" means, so everybody can effin calm down.

I accept that my actions last Friday in the lobby of Laye, Backke and Wacket, Attorneys at Law, 3568 La Benicia Blvd, Los Angeles, California, 90004, were inappropriate and upsetting. I acknowledge Receptionist Lamonia Krinkleton was only doing her job and I didn't really mean what I said about her outfit. Further, contrary to the malicious press release I distributed, I am not producing an S & M movie entitled "**The Bind Side featuring adult film star**

Sandra Fullcock". There is no such production or actress. Finally, I hope my therapist, Dr Florbitz, feels better soon.

December 6   **En Fin**

The tradition of comedy writing – starting in ancient Greece – challenges, pokes fun at and mocks society's most sacred beliefs, its most personal matters.

It is, by its very nature, inappropriate. Aristophanes' plays talk about the relationships among the gods and then makes gleeful, unalloyed fun of those gods. That tradition continues through Chaucer, Shakespeare, Dickens, Molière, Kafka, stand-up comedians and so many others.

The Gwyneth Paltrow vagina candle was a sublime gift, because, like all humor, it's rooted in incongruity. My posts about it "disappointed" some and infuriated others, mostly women, who believed I was being misogynistic. There's a reason I ask somebody to be my social media friend and I hate it if he or she leaves. If however you don't think a candle scented like a human sex organ funny, then we need to part ways.

December 7   **Ready, Fire, Aim**

The Walther PPK is a small, yet extremely powerful, handgun. If I owned one, I'd drive about shooting wind chimes from their porches and perches. They are a crime against humanity and I'm an exceptionally good shot.

December 8

Husbandry, Animal

After mucking horse stalls of a bitter cold afternoon, I found myself herding ducks and an immense goose in a risibly unchoreographed minuet. The din these animals make is a thing of wonder. They mock my herding skills with loud opinions and they're right of course.

In the middle of the fracas, the goose laid a great huge (and warm) egg. When I picked it up, she registered cacophonous displeasure. She does not like me or my ways. The quackers and the honker enjoyed dinner in advance of an animated post-prandial discussion. To know these critters is to know modern political discourse.

December 9

Don't Hate Me Because I'm Beautiful

When my hair gets long, as it is now, I am daily mistaken for bodice-ripper-cover-model Fabio Lanzoni.

"Are you really actor/fashionista/product spokesman Fabio?" women entreat. "Can I touch your hair?" they cry. Or, "Why do you smell of goose?"

Riding a roller coaster more than 20 years ago, a love-sick goose flew into Mr L's chiseled mien. [FL was riding on the roller coaster, not the goose, but accounts differ.]

My rejoinder to such libidinous females is always the same. "Despite my animal magnetism, boyish charm and raw sexuality, I'm merely a humble GE retiree. Also, please don't touch me there." I know their longing however. As Carson McCullers wrote, The Crotch is a Lonely Hunter.

I'm shown wearing the hat of a Pashtun elder. My teeth are not in fact green. They're more of a light teal.

December 10 — Whom Do You Hate?

On a press junket in Poland, during a bus trip, our Soviet Intourist guide couldn't get the arm of her seat up. "How fucking Turkish!" she exclaimed. Everybody hates somebody sometime.

December 11 — You Say Tomato

If you say "Warshington", your usage has a technical term. It's called an intrusive pre-consonantal R. On a map – like most linguistic novelties – you can draw a circle round exactly where it predominates. Now go warsh the dog.

December 12 — Bon Mot

I love words and have spent my long life doing so. If you love words for that long, favorites emerge. My top three includes potvaliant, meaning emboldened by drink. My best and worst decisions are made whilst potvaliant.

December 13 ## My Valet's Wife

Once she surfaced from her cooking sherry-induced delirium, during which she nearly committed a felonious attack on yours truly, Margaret Mary Siobhan Horan was the quintessence of contrition – a charade of course, as she was a deeply depraved woman, consumed by a sea of anger and regret. You'd be too if you were married to my valet, Finial. Since she refuses to divorce, madness is the only recourse. Siobhan is shown a week prior to their nuptials.

December 14 ## Do You Masturbate?

The billionaire college dropout who runs Facebook opened my meager page to The World. I now get friend requests from The Faroe Islands, Azerbaijan, Madagascar, Iran and exotic places too. Some want a pen pal, some a husband, some are selling naughty photos. For a while, I offered nude photos of me, but there were no takers.

These people are sad to learn I'm not that John Oliver. Hey, it makes me sad too. One bold chap from the Middle East demanded to know my sexual orientation and asked if I masturbate. I said I'm a devoted heterosexual and, yes, but not since February.

December 15   **𝕭rain 𝕯rain**

I dined last evening at a swank New Haven, Connecticut, restaurant. Home to Yale, every single human being in that town did way better than me on their SATs, including the busboy. In fact, the busboy – who I discovered is all-but-dissertation in molecular bioengineering – shot me the stink eye whilst I waited for the check. He sensed my paltry education and IQ in the high two figures. Well, young man, my mother smoked when she was pregnant so you can just mind your effin manners.

Smart people think they're better than me, what with their discipline, disposable incomes, net worth, savings, work ethic, luxury cars, MBAs and law degrees, Hollywood-beautiful spouses, giant houses, boats, country clubs, vacations, vacation homes, stocks, bonds, fun neighbors, witty banter, accomplished children and good judgment.

Fuckin' busboy.

December 16   **𝕹egative 𝕮apability**

I stood in the airless little room at the bottom of the Spanish Steps where John Keats died in 1821. He was 26. Just outside, the jangling clamor of Roman life rumbled on. And a deathly silence within. I can't explain it, but it's true.

December 17   Business Progress

The WSJ reported today that since 2018, the General Electric Company has reduced its corporate debt by over US$70 billion. The Hon Leesa Perazzo, my *fiancée*, claims most of that was my expense reports, but that can't be right, can it?

December 18   THREN

My hunched-backed Aunt Marion, a tea-swilling, Woolworth's-loving, doyenne of Albany's Central Avenue, believed the past tense of throw was thren.

> Me: "Aunt Marion, did you see my Time magazine? The one I needed for school?"
> AM: "Oh my land! I thren that out yesterday. Hand me my physic, will ya?"

The only thing between Aunt Marion and perdition was her physic. I once stopped in to see her on the way to Washington when I was trying to get a job in the State Department. "Oh, yeah, them state jobs are swell," Aunt Marion assured me, thinking I sought employment at the DMV. She was wonderful.

December 19   Warmth

My father never used words like bum, hobo or homeless – they were just people "down on their luck". One wintery Sunday, my family dined at Jack's Oyster House in Albany, as we did every Sunday. Just outside the restaurant, a fellow down on his luck asked for spare change. When my father gave him his topcoat, the man cried.

December 20 **One Percenter**

I attended a posh pool party at a posh estate owned by Winthrop Hiram Smith, Jr, whose father was the Smith in Merrill, Lynch, Pierce, Fenner and Smith. The property lived up to the spirit and letter of the word estate – commanding views of lush countryside, an immense and pristine garage home to gleaming classic cars, a vast house of 18th Century dignity with George III silver candelabra scattered about. The Chippendale furniture was period and the ancient mahogany dining room table was roughly the size of the USS Nimitz.

Junior and his wife expanded Winvian Farms, an exotic luxury resort in Morris, Connecticut, near where I lived, and their daughter, Heather, is the managing director. The property, which is, well, posh, features the most elegant treehouse in the world. Winvian is the perfect weekend get-away from the rigours of rolling around in your money.

December 21

Where are the Candles?

Thomas Edison held a huge holiday party the year he invented electric Christmas tree lights. He stuffed everybody who mattered into his swank Manhattan townhouse and they marveled at the brilliant – and safe – tree, at which moment Edison's tabby cat bit into the electric cord, immediately killing the animal and plunging two vast NYC blocks into abject darkness. Merry Christmas.

December 22

Silent, Merry, Happy, Holy, Jolly

The facial hair I now sport is long and black and grey. OK, grey. Note I didn't use the word beard. If I wear my Scottish flat cap, I'm Laird o' th' Manor, but if I wear a trilby hat, the effect is distinctly rabbinic. The other day, a fellow actually asked me to grant a *get* – a divorce – from his wife, which, after reflection, I permitted following some rather shrill testimony. But mostly I'm greeted with, Hey, ya ready for Christmas there, Santa? I've put on extra weight so others can feel better about themselves, my special gift at this magic time of year.

December 23 **Curses, Baby Jesus**

British celebrity chef Jamie Oliver (no relation) allows his five children – this is true – to swear for one minute every Christmas Day. I reckon that's a long minute at *Chez Oliver*.

"This *soi-disant* sole *meunière* is a steaming pile of dog shit, Dad!" said an agitated 9-year-old Petal Blossom Rainbow Oliver last year. "Where are the fucking profiteroles already?" she continued.

If you have little ones in your family, you should give them an unfettered minute of vulgarity on the 25th just like the Olivers. Their grandparents will laugh and laugh.

December 24 **The Good Olde World**

In early 19th Century England – and before – Christmas was deeply unpopular, an excuse, it was thought, for the lower orders to drink and debauch. You can hear the contempt in Scrooge's voice when he says, "I suppose you'll want the whole day off." Cratchit brags of excess, two full rounds of gin punch for his wife and children. The next day, he's hung-over and late to work. "I am behind my time, Sir," he tells Scrooge in apology. "I was *making rather merry*." The story almost never got written.

Dickens wanted to write a hectoring pamphlet on the horrors of child labor, which he experienced in a boot-blacking (shoe polish) factory. His publisher had a better idea and that's how **A Christmas Carol** came to be. It was an appeal for kindness over greed, of charity over gain. It was, and is, Liberal versus Conservative, truth versus fiction. Welcome to 1843 – and to our epoch too.

December 25   **cA Tradition**

I've shared this quote for decades. The passage is not from **A Christmas Carol** (1843), as you'd expect, but from **The Pickwick Papers** (1836). I hope today finds you by your own fireside and your quiet home.

We write these words now, many miles distant from the spot at which, year after year, we met on that day, a merry and joyous circle. Many of the hearts that throbbed so gaily then have ceased to beat; many of the looks that shone so brightly then have ceased to glow; the hands we grasped have grown cold; the eyes we sought have hid their lustre in the grave; and yet the old house, the room, the merry voices and smiling faces, the jest, the laugh, the most minute and trivial circumstances connected with those happy meetings, crowd upon our mind at each recurrence of the season, as if the last assemblage had been but yesterday! Happy, happy Christmas, that can win us back to the delusions of our childish days, that can recall to the old man the pleasures of his youth, that can transport the sailor and the traveller, thousands of miles away, back to his own fireside and his quiet home!

– Charles Dickens, The Pickwick Papers, 1836

December 26   **Give till it Hurts**

I volunteered at a swank and glittering charity event a few nights ago. My tasks were light and simple. Thirty minutes before the show began plates of fruit, crackers, cheese and grapes were set out for the volunteers. Off to the very distant side of the table, alone, was a plate of brownies covered in three layers of aluminum foil. I go weak in the knees for good brownies, so I ate four.

In 15 minutes, I felt strange and at 25 minutes, I was stoned as a goat, profoundly incoherently stoned, baked, as the young people say. I muddled – stumbled really – through my tasks then mumbled my need to decamp at the quick march. I regard pot as a crude drug, not fit for civilized society. My evening reinforced that view.

December 27   **Stepfather**

After GE Capital, I worked as a stable hand in a Newtown barn. One cold December night, the pregnant mare decided it was time. She struggled, running about the stall wildly; I pulled the foal from her as the owners, in

Florida, watched on closed circuit TV. Mother and child were fine, and the colt was named Oliver. I was so proud. He's shown napping, among the core competencies all Olivers share.

December 28   Cabin Crew Prepare for Landing

At Seagram and even more at GE, I traveled at will and my trips were always foreign. In GE speak, I was OOC. Out of Country suggested, but did not always entail, great purpose. Some junkets were serious – a crisis, acquisition or imbroglio that might make news.

But often there wasn't a purpose at all, except escape. From Kennedy, I'd call my best friend to casually say, "Well, I'm off to Bucharest." The bartender at The Connaught knew my kids' names. I had a Harley Street physician. In India, the concierge greeted me with a familiar smile. A posh Zurich hotel printed business cards I could use in town.

Now, much later, you see, I'm haunted. I should have been home. Now when there's nowhere to go.

December 29   Career Choice

On a deep winter night, I slept in a gilded Polish castle. I consumed caviar on the Concorde while watching the curvature of the Earth. Work twice brought me to the Oval Office, the second visit a messy business. I drank Sauterne and ate *foie gras* at breakfast. At the *Cafe de la Paix*, on an elegant summer evening and to the delight of my companion, a Parisian pigeon shit on my suit, new from Savile Row. I was a guest of HRH Prince Philip on HMY Britannia.

I mystified everyday Londoners by waving regally to them from the back of a giant Daimler-Benz. In Germany, my speech – in German – got intended laughs from the natives. Eating char caught an hour before well above the Arctic Circle invigorates. On a summer day, I stood alone in what Shakespeare called the vasty fields of France.

For three years, I battled the Hungarian parliament to a draw. Early one morning, in India, the Arabian Sea gleamed unforgettably in the South Asian sun. I always urge a career in PR on young people. It's much more entertaining than actual work.

December 30 — **The Pledge of Allegiance**

Each morning before the school bus arrived, Winifred Smith Oliver, our mother, would douse my brother and me

with so much Vitalis Hair Tonic For Men we could have qualified as Superfund Sites. A rigorous cleaning of our ear canals with Q-Tips preceded the tsunami of Vitalis.

Clip-on ties around our necks, we scampered to the front of The Pink Palace to await Walt, the taciturn driver and his yellow bus. Our lunch boxes jangled in the outbound and in-bound segments of our daily journey. With us gone at 7:50 am every day, Winifred Smith Oliver would begin drinking in earnest.

December 31   Start Your Engines

New Year's Eve, 1999, I attended a glittering black tie party in Scarsdale, NY. At the time, I was a spokesman for GE Capital, a vast financial services group. We owned banks round the globe and worried people might be cranky when our ATMs froze.

We were told of the cataclysm that awaited ("Your cars won't start on New Year's Day, " the IT experts warned). It was called Y2K. Because everything would fail, I'd been outfitted with advanced communications equipment on an elaborate belt round my waist and over my cummerbund – seven different devices. I looked like Batman.

My company had conference calls through the night, starting with the South Pacific Islands. Each hour, we moved farther west. Given the utter absence of cataclysm and the increased consumption of Champagne, our meetings became more robust. In the last one, after the US East Coast, we sang Auld Lang Syne. Not well, but with vigour.

JPV Oliver, Gent, is a writer whose work has appeared in The Albany Times-Union, The Newtown Connecticut Bee, Philadelphia Weekly and Newsweek. He is a recipient of the prestigious Laphroaig Prize for Literature. Oliver and his wife, The Hon Leesa Perazzo, summer in Saratoga Springs, NY. They February there too.

Lightning Source UK Ltd.
Milton Keynes UK
UKHW020316230322
400389UK00007B/164/J